Spelling and phonics

Light

PHOTOCOPIABLES

impact

WRITING HOMEWORK

Published by Scholastic Ltd,
Villiers House,
Clarendon Avenue,
Leamington Spa,
Warwickshire CV32 5PR

© 1996 Scholastic Ltd
1 2 3 4 5 6 7 8 9 0 6 7 8 9 0 1 2 3 4 5
Text © 1996 University of
North London Enterprises Ltd

UNIVERSITY OF
NORTH LONDON

Activities by the IMPACT Project at the University of North London, collated and rewritten by Ruth Merttens, Alan Newland, Susie Webb

Editor Jane Bishop
Assistant editor Ben Orme
Designer Toby Long
Series designer Anna Oliwa
Illustrations Martin Cater
Cover illustration Headlines, Charlbury, Oxford

Designed using Aldus Pagemaker
Printed in Great Britain by Clays Ltd,
Bungay, Suffolk

British Library Cataloguing-in-Publication Data
A catalogue record for this book is available from the British Library.

ISBN 0-590 53373-8

All rights reserved. This book is sold subject to the condition that it shall not, by way of trade or otherwise, be lent, hired out or otherwise circulated without the publisher's prior consent in any form of binding or cover other rthan that in which it is published and without a similar condition, including this condition, being imposed upon the subsequent purchaser.

No part of this publication may be reproduced, stored in a retrieval system, or transmitted, in any form or by any means, electronic, mechanical, photocopying, recording or otherwise, without the prior permission of the publisher. This book remains copyright, although permission is granted to copy pages 6 to 10, 13 to 48; 51 to 88 and 91 to 128 for classroom distribution and use only in the school which has purchased the book, or by the teacher who has purchased this book and in accordance with the CLA licensing agreement. Photocopying permission is given for purchasers only and not for borrowers of books from any lending service.

KEY STAGE ONE
CONTENTS

Introduction	5	Teddy names	39
Parents' letter	6	Animal magic	40
Parents' booklet	7–10	Messy me	41
		Wilf walking	42
Reception		Which letter	43
Teachers' notes	11–12	Drum beats	44
Letter count	13	Initial names	45
Memory sounds	14	Beginning and end	46
Touching toys	15	But I'm not too tired	47
Name pictures	16	Cartoon character	48
Kitchen	17		
Name labels	18	**Year One**	
Labels for schools	19	Teachers' notes	49–50
Mars landing	20	Word use	51
Family album	21	Peng-aroo	52
Picture rhymes	22	Rhyme detective	53
Unusual initial	23	Letter search	54
Animal starter	24	Cereal word hunt	55
Name rhyme	25	Alphabet animals	56
Vehicle starter	26	'Cr' hunt	57
Alphabet choice	27	'St' hunt	58
Alphabet sequence	28	'Fl' hunt	59
Alphabet wheel	29	Baby talk	60
Family and friends	30	Last name animals	61
Back to front	31	Moving letters	62
Letter portrait	32	Sound sums	63
Opposite ends	33	Alphabet vehicles	64
Only two	34	Fat cat small ball	65
Y words	35	Number rhymes	66
Street names	36	Animal names	67
Place names	37	Days of the week	68
Pet names	38	Body parts	69

impact
WRITING HOMEWORK

KEY STAGE ONE
CONTENTS

Address labels	70
Mixed numbers	71
Emotional sounds	72
Greetings	73
Fare-thee-well	74
End of the line	75
Gift tags	76
Abracadabra!	77
Illuminated letters	78
Turn about	79
Alphabet names	80
Coded alphabet	81
Code names	82
Secret names	83
Backward name	84
Common words	85
Newspaper alphabet	86
Three letter guess	87
Station names	88

Year Two
Teachers' notes	89–90
Breakfast words	91
Silly sentences	92
Silent letters	93
Onomatopoeia	94
Collecting 'ing'	95
Do-ing at home	96
'Two, to or too?'	97
A hoard of boards	98
Fright night!	99
Eeeek!	100
Word chains	101
Food word chain	102
Animal word chain	103
Verb word chain	104
Adjective word chain	105
Forget-me-not	106
Four letter word chain	107
Colour rhymes	108
Hobby words	109
Blended sounds	110
Syllable count up	111
Mixed teens	112
Word stairs	113
Moon	114
Suffix	115
Phone shop!	116
Tele-tele	117
Double o	118
Rhyming animals	119
Rhyming sentence	120
Star light star bright	121
Spellcheck	122
Valentine message	123
Dragon's teeth	124
Newspaper words	125
Spot the missing letters	126
More than one	127
Afterword	128

impact
WRITING HOMEWORK

IMPACT INTRODUCTION

IMPACT books are designed to help teachers involve parents in children's learning to write. Through the use of interesting and specially developed writing tasks, parents can encourage and support their child's efforts as they become confident and competent writers.

The shared writing programme is modelled on the same process as the IMPACT shared maths which encompasses a non-traditional approach to homework.

This is outlined in the following diagram:

> The teacher selects a task based on the work she is doing in class. The activity may relate to the children's work in a particular topic, to the type of writing they are engaged in or to their reading.

⇩

> The teacher prepares the children for what they have to do at home. This may involve reading a particular story, playing a game or having a discussion with the children about the task.

⇩

> The children take home the activity, and share it with someone at home. This may be an older brother/sister, a parent or grandparent or any other friend or relation.

⇩

> The parents and children respond to the activity by commenting in an accompanying diary or notebook.
> * This mechanism provides the teacher with valuable feedback.

⇩

> The teacher uses what was done at home as the basis for follow-up work in class. This may involve further writing, drawing, reading or discussion.

The activities in this book have been designed to enable children to develop and expand their writing skills in conversation with those at home. Where possible the activities reflect the context of the home rather than the school, and draw upon experiences and events from out-of-school situations.

Shared activities – or homework with chatter!

Importantly, the activities are designed to be shared. Unlike traditional homework, where the child is expected to 'do it alone' and not to have help, with IMPACT they are encouraged – even required – to find someone to talk to and share the activity with. With each task we say the following should be true:

- something is said;
- something is written;
- something is read.

Sometimes the main point of the IMPACT activity is the discussion – and so we do try to encourage parents to see that the task involves a lot more than just completing a piece of writing. It is very important that teachers go through the task carefully with the children so that they know what to do. Clearly not all the children, or parents, will be able to read the instructions in English and so this preparation is crucial if the children are to be able to share the activity. The sheet often acts more as a backup or a prompt than a recipe.

Diaries

The shared writing works by involving parents in their children's learning. The IMPACT diaries* are a crucial part of this process. They provide a mechanism by means of which an efficient parent-teacher-dialogue is established. These diaries enable teachers to obtain valuable feedback both about children's performances in relation to specific activities and about the tasks themselves. Parents are able to alert the teacher to any matter of concern or pleasant occurrences, and nothing is left to come as a big surprise or a horrible shock in the end of year report. It is difficult to exaggerate the importance of the IMPACT diaries. The OFSTED inspectors and HMI have highly commended their effectiveness in helping to raise children's achievements and in developing a real partnership with parents.
* See the Afterword (page 128) for details of where to obtain these.

Timing

Most schools send the Shared Writing activities fortnightly. Many interleave these activities with the IMPACT maths tasks, thus ensuring that the children have something to share with their parents almost every week. Many schools also use the shared writing tasks to enhance their shared reading or PACT programme. It has been found that some parents may be encouraged to take a renewed interest in reading a book with their child on a regular basis when the shared writing project is launched in a class. However, there are a variety of practices and the important point is that each teacher should feel comfortable with how often IMPACT is sent in her class.

Parent friendly

It is important for the success of the IMPACT Shared Writing that parents are aware of both the purpose and the extent of each activity. Many teachers adopt a developmental approach to writing, encouraging emergent writing or the use of invented spellings. Care has to be taken to share the philosophy behind this approach with parents, and to select activities which will not assume that parents are as familiar with the implications as teachers. You will get lots of support if parents can see that what they are doing is helping their child to become cheerful and successful writers!

To facilitate this process, each activity contains a note to parents which helps to make it clear what the purpose of the activity is, and how they can best help. The activities also contain hints to help parents share the activity in an enjoyable and effective manner. Sometimes the hints contain ideas, or starting points. On other occasions they may be examples or demonstrations of how to set about the task concerned.

It is always important to bear in mind that parents can, and sometimes should, do things differently at home. At home, many children will enjoy, and even benefit from, copying underneath a line of text or writing without paying attention to spelling or punctuation, where in school such things might not be expected or encouraged. The most successful partnerships between home and school recognise both the differences and the similarities in each other's endeavours.

Planning

The shared writing activities are divided into three sections according to age: Reception, Year 1 and Year 2. There are two pages of teachers' notes relating to the individual activities at the beginning

of each section. When selecting which activity to send home with the children it is helpful to remember the following:
- Ideally, we send the same activity with each child in the class or year. The activities are mostly designed to be as open-ended as possible, to allow for a wide variety of different levels of response. Teachers often add a few extra comments of their own to a particular sheet to fit it to the needs of a particular child or group of children with special educational needs. It is also important to stress that the child does not have to do all the actual writing – often the parent does half or more. The point of the activity may lie in the discussion and the creation of a joint product.
- It is useful to send a variety of different activities. Some children will particularly enjoy a word game, while others will prefer a task which includes drawing a picture. Activities may be used to launch a topic, to support a particular project, to enable a good quality of follow-up to an idea and to revise or practise particular skills. Much of the benefit of the shared writing exercise may be derived from the follow-up work back in the classroom. Therefore, it is very important to select activities which will feed into the type of work being focused upon at that time. For example, if the class is working on grammatical categories, verbs, nouns, etc., then an activity requiring that children and parents produce real and fictional definitions of long words will fit in well. On the other hand, if the class is doing some work on fairy stories, making a **wanted** poster of a character in a story may be appropriate.

Notes to teachers

These give suggestions to the teachers. They outline what may be done before the activity is sent to ensure that it goes well at home. And they describe how the activity may be followed up as part of routine classwork during the subsequent week. More help with what happens when the activity comes back is to be found in the Afterword on page 128.

Parent letter and booklet

It is very important that parents are kept informed about the nature of this new-style homework. Most schools elect to launch IMPACT Shared Writing by having a meeting or a series of meetings. We have included here a draft letter to parents and a booklet which schools may photocopy and give to parents. The booklet is eight A5 pages when copied, folded and collated. This can be given to all new parents as their children start school. There is a space on the cover for the school name.

Keeping shared writing going...

There are a few tips which have been found over the years to make life simpler for parents, teachers and children:
- Don't send shared writing activities in the first few weeks of the September term. Shared writing, like IMPACT maths, usually starts in the third week of the new school year.
- Don't send shared writing activities in the second half of the summer term. Shared writing, like IMPACT maths, usually belongs to the heart of the school year.
- Do value the work that the children and their parents do at home. Sometimes it may not be presented as you expect – for example, a lot of parents with young children write in upper case rather than lower case letters or will ask children to **write over** a line of print. Remember that what comes back into class is a starting point for work that you consider appropriate, and is facilitating both discussion and partnership.

Dear Parents,

In our class, we have decided to use a new 'shared homework scheme' designed to help develop and improve children's writing skills. This will involve sending home a regular task in the form of an A4 sheet. The sheet will outline a simple writing activity for you and your child to enjoy together. These are designed to be shared; the children are not expected to complete the tasks alone.

We would very much like to talk to you about this scheme, and so on _____ we shall hold three short meetings. You need only come to **one** of these and can choose the time which is most convenient:
- 9.00 in the morning
- 3.30 in the afternoon
- 7.00 in the evening.

We would really like as many parents as possible to attend.

Your help in supporting your child's learning is a crucial part of his/her success at school. We do appreciate the time and trouble that parents take with their children, and we can certainly see the benefits in the quality of the children's work and the enthusiasm with which they attack it.

Please return the slip at the bottom of the letter.

Yours sincerely,

_____

Name _____   Class _____

I would like to attend the meeting at:

9.00 in the morning

3.30 in the afternoon

7.00 in the evening

Please tick **one** time only.

Don't forget...

Pick your time!
When you both want to do the activity.

Don't over-correct!
This can be very discouraging.

Your child does not always have to do all the writing!
You may take turns, or take over sometimes.

Make it fun!
If either of you gets tired or bored help a bit more. Tasks should not last more than 20 minutes unless you want them to!

Praise and encourage as much as you can!

IMPACT

Shared Writing

SPIKE

School name

_____

About Shared Writing

- The teacher selects an activity.
- The teacher explains the activity to the class.
- Child and helper read through the activity.
- Child and helper talk about the activity.
- Child and helper share the writing.
- Child and helper comment on the activity in the diary.
- Child brings the activity back into school.
- Teacher reads the comments in the diary.
- The teacher follows up the activity in class.

Spelling and punctuation

We all agree that correct spelling and punctuation are very important. However........

DO

- Notice punctuation when sharing the writing activity.
- Talk about different uses of capital and lower case letters.
- Play word games such as 'I spy' or 'Hangman'.
- Read what the child has written before you make any comment about spelling, punctuation or presentation.
- Help them learn any words sent home by the school.

DON'T

- Worry about every mistake – children can become very anxious about their writing if constantly interrupted.
- With young children don't insist that they spell every word correctly. At this stage we are encouraging them to 'be writers'.
- Don't worry if your child is quite slow to learn to spell and punctuate – these things come with time and encouragement.

How we write

Writing also has a mechanical side, children have to learn to form their letters, to separate words, to begin and end sentences.

When children are first learning to write it can be very discouraging to be constantly corrected. However, as they become more confident, we can afford to draw their attention to these things:

Starting school

Your child already knows quite a lot about writing when they start........

They may

- be able to tell the difference between writing and pictures;

- realise that writing has words and spaces;

- know some letters of their name;

- be able to make marks on paper or form a few letters;

- understand that 'talk' can be written down and that writing can give messages or information;

- know that we write from left to right in English;

- play at 'reading' their own 'writing'.

Being a writer...

Is about...
Having ideas
Composing them
Communicating them

WANTED
A Purpose
a.k.a.
A Greeting
A Compliment
An Enquiry
A Gossip
A Thought.

To An Audience
my teacher
mum or Dad
Friend or foe
Near or far

Choose from our catalogue of Types of Writing
a letter
a poster
a list
a book

Parents can help by...

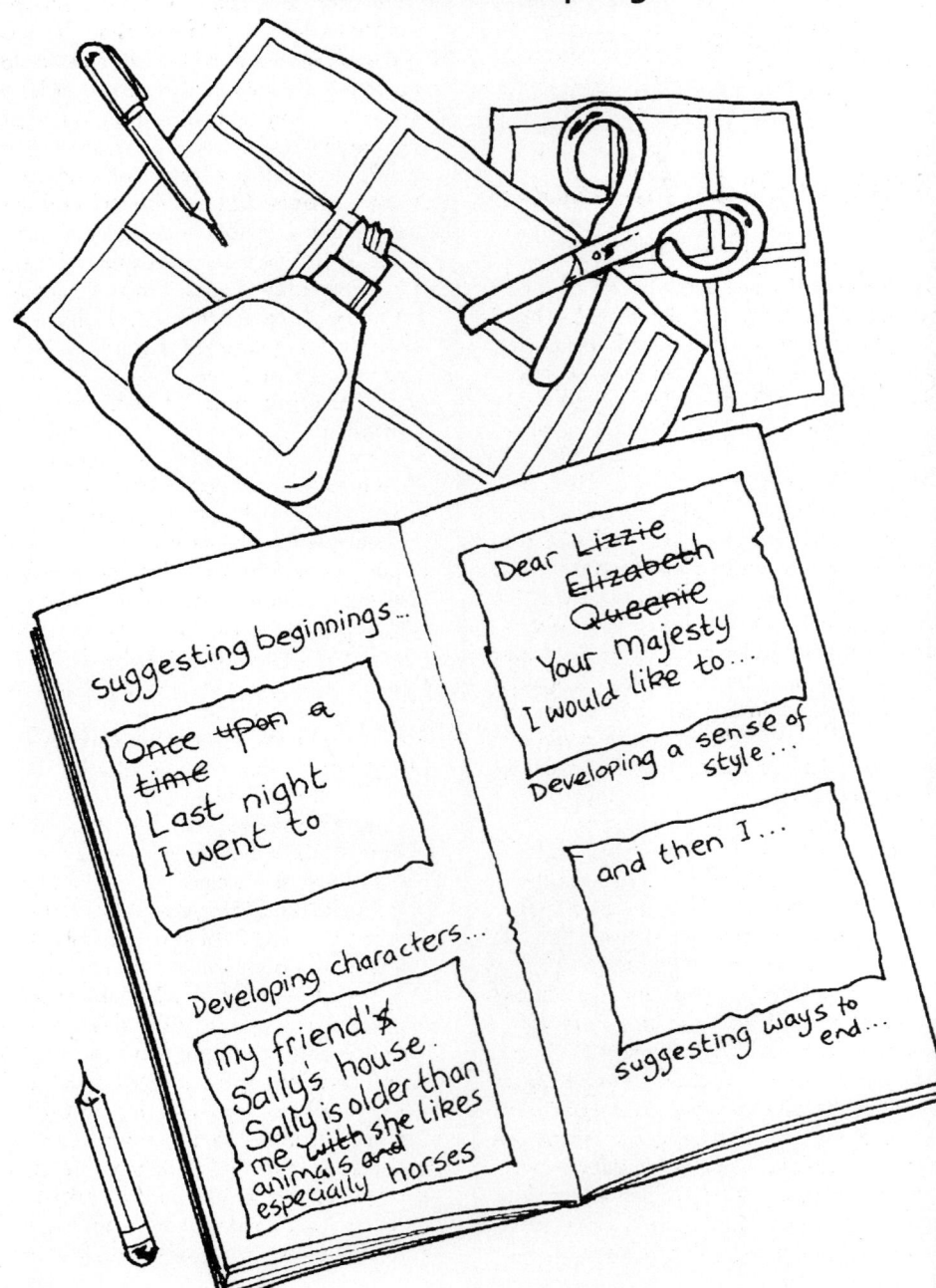

Suggesting beginnings...
~~Once upon a time~~
Last night I went to

Dear ~~Lizzie~~ ~~Elizabeth~~ ~~Queenie~~ Your Majesty
I would like to...

Developing a sense of style...
and then I...

suggesting ways to end...

Developing characters...
My friend's Sally's house.
Sally is older than me ~~with~~ she likes animals ~~and~~ especially horses

Teachers' Notes
RECEPTION

Letter count Does everyone know the names of the letters? Make alphabet books with the children. Write a letter on each page and the children can practise writing the letter and draw a picture or several pictures of things that start with that letter on each one.

Memory sounds Display the pictures the children have drawn; or get them to paint larger versions that can be displayed as an alphabet frieze around the classroom. Write the letter *and* the name of the object in the picture by each one. If you have a child-level display board you could display the pictures all over the board, alongside all of the letters in a group with some pins or Blu-Tack. The children can then pin or stick the letters to the appropriate pictures.

Touching toys Make sets of toys according to their initial letter. For example, collect up all the boats, balls, bears etc. You can match the sets to the alphabet on the wall. Talk about the toys that begin with the same letter as the child's name. You can extend this activity by counting the *number* of letters in each toy's name and categorising them this way.

Name pictures Display the name pictures in a book that the children can pick up and read for themselves. Perhaps the children can make alphabet zigzag books and use the other children's ideas for different animals for each letter. Which letters don't you have animals for? Together can you think of animals to fill the gaps?

Kitchen Did anyone think of kitchen utensils for each letter? Try some different acrostics with the children, using the name of their favourite toys, for example. Help the children think of describing words, or words for things they like to do with their toy. Do this altogether or in a small group as it is quite difficult for this age group.

Name labels/Labels for school Ensure the children can spell their names correctly. Make sure the labels are legible; these can be used to label books, drawers, pegs, lunchboxes, etc. As the children have written them themselves this will make them far more recognisable.

Mars landing These Martians will make a wonderful display. Talk to the children about their pictures and the names they have invented. Talk about the letters they have chosen; pick out any phonetic connections the children have made. Talk about the importance of 'having a go' at spellings – using what you know about letters to guess spellings. Make Martians out of Plasticine or clay. Write big book stories with small groups of children that they can then read themselves.

Family album 'Frame' the children's pictures and mount them in a class 'family album' that the children can read – or display them on the wall. Ask the children to explain their pictures and read the names under the pictures. If you are going to do a wall display, you could ask the children to bring in photos of family members to go with their pictures. The children could make small books about their families writing a short descriptive sentence on each page with a picture eg. 'Dad loves playing on my Nintendo' or 'Mum reading a book with me'.

Picture rhymes Look at everyone's pictures together. If the pictures are clear enough, you could just read half the rhyme, and see if the children can guess the end. Talk about how (most) of the rhymes have matching endings eg. -ig, ot, -og, etc. Prepare some pictures like the children's (maybe use their ideas). Write next to each picture the rhyme. Get the children to underline the part that rhymes each time.

Unusual initial Discuss the children's ideas, who has thought of the most unusual thing? Display all the pictures together on the wall, with the children's names next to the pictures. Get the children to write capital and small A's in their books. Let the children continue with this activity using the first letter of their name.

Animal starter Read out all the children's ideas. Paint pictures of them. Perhaps the children can make alphabet zigzag books and use the other children's ideas for different animals for each letter. Which letters don't you have animals for? Can you think of any that could fill the gaps?

Name rhyme Look at everyone's sentences together; can the children guess the ends of the rhymes? Talk about how most of the rhymes have 'matching' endings eg. -en, -ie, -er, etc. Prepare some pictures of children doing actions that rhyme with their names. Write the rhyme next to each picture. Get the children to underline the part that rhymes each time.

Vehicle starter Get the children to share their ideas. Draw pictures of their vehicle starters and display them with appropriate labels; for example 'Rebecca's rocket', or 'Helen's helicopter', etc. Read the labels. Talk about apostrophe s ('s) and what it means. Can you sort the ideas into alphabetical order? Which letters of the alphabet are missing?

Alphabet choice Collect the children's favourite letters together. Put the letters in order. Where are the gaps? Get the children to write their favourite letter again in the middle of a sheet of paper (or you could do it for them). Can they think of some things or names that start with that letter? To start the children off, go through some of the sounds and give them some ideas. If this is too confusing for your class, concentrate on *one* initial for everyone at a time.

Alphabet sequence Have the children written their letters as capitals or small letters? Whose name is the first/last in the alphabet? Sort the letters. Can anyone think of a good way to sort them? For example: all the letters with a circle as part of the letters (a, b, c, d, e, g, o, p, q) and all the letters without; all the letters with a 'stick' – long 'sticks' or short 'sticks' a b d f g h i j k l m n p q r t u y (those with the circles having short 'sticks').

Alphabet wheel Play this in school before you send it home. Photocopy and enlarge the Alphabet wheel and stick it up on a board. Choose a few players and give them a counter and a blob of Blu-tack each to secure the counters. Use a large dice. When the children move around the board, say the letters as you pass them. The players can either think of a word themselves that starts with that letter or they choose sometime else to think of one for them. Talk about where the letters are on the track and the order that they go in.

Family and friends Discuss the children's lists. Who has written theirs in capitals and whose is written in small letters? Does anyone's name start with the letter 'a'? Whose name comes last in the alphabet? Which is the most common letter? Can anyone think of a good way to sort them?

Back to front Try this activity in school first. Try thinking of as many three letter words as you can. Maybe you could start the children off with the 'sound' of the word and they could find as many rhyming versions as they can, for example: can/pan/fan/Dan/Jan etc. Display the children's pictures on the wall. Has anyone found any *real* words by reading their word back to front?

impact WRITING HOMEWORK

Spelling and phonics

Letter portrait Look at the children's letters. Look out for capitals and small letters. Which is the most common? Can anyone think of a good way to sort them?

Opposite ends Look at the children's ideas. Have they had difficulty finding 'z' words? Who has thought of the most unusual 'z' word? Chant through the alphabet together. What are the letters in the middle of the alphabet? Can you put them in order together?

Only two Words that have only two letters can be easily guessed if the sounds of the letters are known. List the words the children bring in and see if anyone can read them back. Look at the letters in the words and talk about the 'sounds' the letters make. Emphasise the difference between a 'letter' and a 'word'. Cut the words out and stick them on to the side of a board with Blu-tack. Write out a few sentences with the two letter words missing and ask the children to fill the gap.

'Y' words Talk through a few examples in school first; emphasise the 'ee' sound that 'y' usually makes at the end of a word. See if anyone has managed to find any words where the 'y' does not have an 'ee' sound. Get the children to draw pictures to depict the adjectives which they have found.

Street names Look at all the street names the children bring in. Does anyone live in the same street as anyone else? Look at the first letters of the street names. Can any of the children match the initial letter of their street name with anyone else's? Look at the fact that street names, along with any other kind of name, always start with a capital letter. Has anyone written their name like a real street sign, all in capital letters? Look at the different ways of saying 'streets', for example: Avenue, Close, Way or Road. Does anyone live down a street that just has a name, for example: The Orchards?

Place names Look at all the place names the children bring in. Does everyone live in the same village, town or city as everyone else or not? Look at the first letters of the place names. Discuss how place names, along with any other kind of name, always *start* with a capital letter.

Pet names Look at the first letters of the pet names. Can any of the children match the initial letter of their pet name with anyone else's? Look at the fact that pet names, along with any other kind of name, always start with a capital letter. How do the names fit the animals? For example: 'Smoky' for a grey cat or 'Rover' for a dog. Can the children guess one another's animals from their names? Display all the children's drawings of their pets. Sort the pets into different groups of animals.

Teddy names Read a Paddington story with the children first and discuss how he got his name. Look at all the teddy names. Does anyone have the same teddy name as anyone else? Can the children match the initial letter of their teddy name with anyone else's? Look at the fact that teddy names, along with any other kind of name, always start with a capital letter. Ask the children how their teddies got their names. Can they remember how Paddington got his? Count how many letters are in each name and sort the names again (for this it might be useful to have the names printed out on card).
A Bear called Paddington, Michael Bond (Young Lions)

Animal magic Collect the children's pictures of animals, and what they say together. Read a few of them with the children. Slowly point to each sound as you read it, emphasising which letters make which sounds. Talk about the fact that pictures that go with writing can often help us predict what the words are going to say. Display the children's pictures and encourage the children to tell one another what their animal is saying.

Messy me Get the children to 'read out' their describing words and show their pictures. Has anyone used the initial blend in their name in their describing word? For example: 'Freezing Fred' or 'Glum Gloria'. Choose a few of the children's names and try to think of other words that begin with that sound. Can you make a silly sentence using the name, the adjective and a few other words? Write the sentence near the picture and ask the children to underline the initial letter that is the same throughout the sentence. Emphasise the fact that not all the words start with the same sound.

Wilf walking Read out some of the children's ideas. Has anyone used the initial blend in their name in their doing word? For example: 'Brishty breathing'. Choose a few of the children's names and try to think of other words that begin with that sound. Can you make a silly sentence, using the name, verb and a few other words? For example: 'Jumping Julie just jumped over the jam jar'. Get the children to illustrate their silly sentences. Write the sentences near the pictures, and ask the children to underline the initial letter that is the same throughout the sentence. Emphasise the fact that the words don't necessarily start with the same sound.

Which letter? Use an alphabet frieze to help you chant through the alphabet together in school. Did the children know that there were 26 letters in the alphabet? Once the children bring back their work, put the names and initial letters in order, starting from number one. Does anyone's name begin with 'A'? Whose name comes last in the alphabet? Which letter is most common? Talk about the orders of letters in the alphabet – refer to the order first, second, third etc.

Drum beats Try this activity out in the classroom with teacher's names *before* you send it home. When the children bring back the activity, sit them in a circle and take it in turns to clap out and say their names. Does anyone have a matching number of claps? For example: 'An-nie' (bang bang), 'Sus-ie' (bang bang). How many children only have one syllable in their name? Who has the largest number of syllables in their name? Can everyone clap out the longest name?

Initial names What is the most common initial in your class? Write a list of all the names with the most common initial. How many boys names are there? How many girls names are there? What are the children's favourite names? Has anyone chosen names of people in their families or from stories they know?

Beginning and end Choose one of the children's names to talk about. What letter does it start with? What does it end with? Write the name on the board. Underline the first and last letters and divide the boards into two halves, i.e. Ricardo R/O. Ask the children what words they can think of starting with either of those two letters.

But I'm not tired Before the activity goes home, read *Whatever Next* by Jill Murphy (Walker Books) with the children and talk about the long story which Baby Bear made up so that he didn't have to go straight upstairs and get in his bath. Also try *Aren't You Tired, Little Bear?* (Walker Books). When the children bring back their excuses, talk about them. Has anyone's excuse ever worked? Who has the most outrageous excuse?

Cartoon character Write all the cartoon character names on the board or on a sheet that all the children can see. Does anyone have the same favourite cartoon character as anyone else? Can anyone spot matching initial sounds? Give those children a special pen to underline the matching sounds. What is the most common initial letter? Can you place the names in alphabetical order?

Letter count

- How many different letters can you write?
- Write them down, and try to count them.
- Can you write any letters from your name?

To the helper:

- Start with any letters your child knows (for example the first letters in their name).
- Talk about the letters they have written, what things can they think of that start with that sound? Add you own ideas.
- You could write down some words you both think of.

The first letters in a child's name are often the first ones they learn. Finding other things that start with those letters draws on their natural interest in them. Learning to discriminate between letters and to write each letter is a vital step in learning to write.

_____and

child

_____

helper(s)

_____

did this activity together

impact WRITING HOMEWORK

Spelling and phonics

To the helper:

- Talk about the sound your child has chosen, what things can they think of that start with that sound? Help out with some ideas of your own.
- If your child wants, you could write down some of the words you both think of.

Learning the relationship between how a letter sounds and how it looks is an important stage in writing development.

_____and
child

_____
helper(s)

_____
did this activity together

Memory sounds

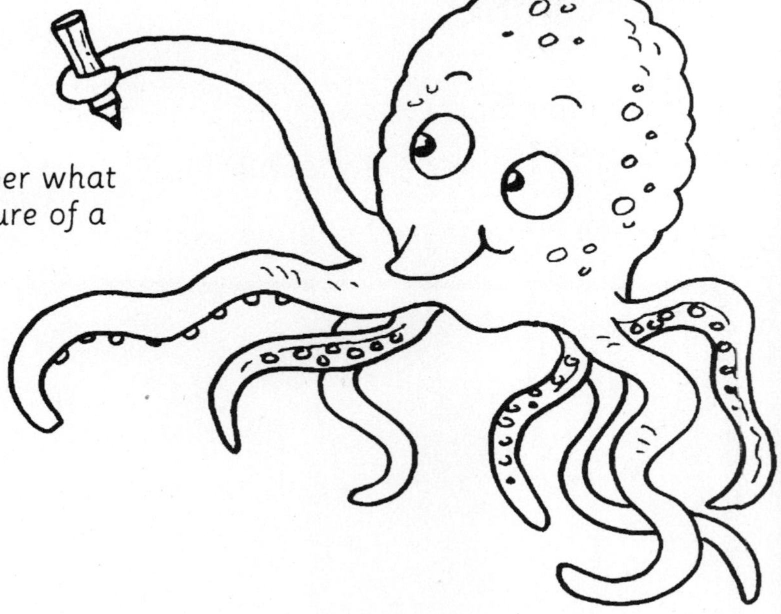

- Write down a letter.

- Draw a picture that will help you remember what sound that letter makes (for example a picture of a bat for b, a picture of an octopus for o).

impact WRITING HOMEWORK

14   **Spelling and phonics**

Touching toys

● Draw a toy that starts with the same sound as your name.

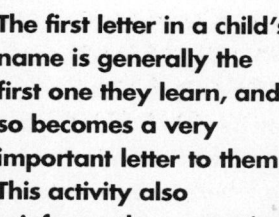

To the helper:

● Talk about your child's initial letter, and try to think of a range of things (not necessarily toys) that start with that letter.
● Let your child draw a picture of a toy, and if they want they could try to write its name down. If not, you could do the writing, and then you can talk about the letters that *match*.

The first letter in a child's name is generally the first one they learn, and so becomes a very important letter to them. This activity also reinforces the connection between how a letter sounds and how it looks which is an important stage for your child.

_____and
child

_____
helper(s)

_____
did this activity together

impact WRITING HOMEWORK   **Spelling and phonics** 15

To the helper:

- Help your child write their name if necessary.
- If a very long name, use the shorter version!
- Talk about the sound each letter makes, and think of a few animals; a tiger, tortoise etc.. Get the child to draw the one they like next to the letter.
- Write the name of each animal next to their picture.

The letters in a child's name are important ones for them and usually the first they learn. This activity helps them learn their initial sounds through the letters in their name. Learning to discriminate between letters and to write each letter of the alphabet is a vital first step in learning to write.

_____and

child

_____

helper(s)

_____

did this activity together

16 **Spelling and phonics**

Name pictures

- Write down your first name.

- Look at each letter in your name, and draw a picture of an animal to go with each one.

impact WRITING HOMEWORK

Kitchen

● Think of a word to go with each letter in **kitchen**.

We have suggested the first word.

k itten
i
t
c
h
e
n

To the helper:

● Try filling in words for the letters which your child can work out first, and then help with the others. For example, if your child gets stuck on the letter **i**, suggest a few ideas of **i** words, as examples.
● Help with the writing if necessary.

This activity gives the children experience in hunting for words that begin with specific letters. Learning initial sounds will help them when they are both reading and writing.

_____and
child

_____
helper(s)

_____
did this activity together

Spelling and phonics

To the helper:

- If your child is not sure about how to write his/her name, you could write the first label.
- Talk about the letters in their name; do they know what they are called, and what sound they make?

The letters in a child's name are the most important ones to them, as they are usually the first they learn. This activity will help children remember how to write their name, and to recognise it.

_____and

child

_____

helper(s)

_____

did this activity together

18 Spelling and phonics

Name labels

- Use these five labels. Can you write your name on them?
- Now decorate them.

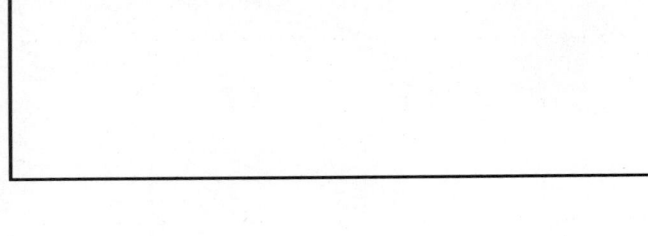

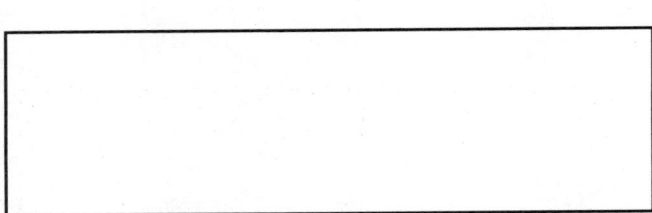

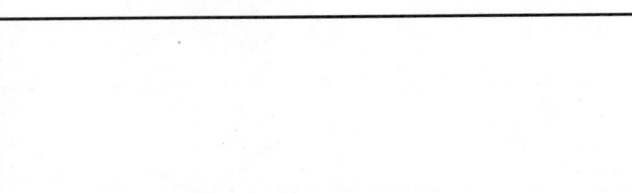

- Label five things in your house with your labels.

Make sure you can spell your name on your own!

impact WRITING HOMEWORK

Labels for school

- Use these labels and write your first and second name clearly on each one.

Make sure you spell them both right!

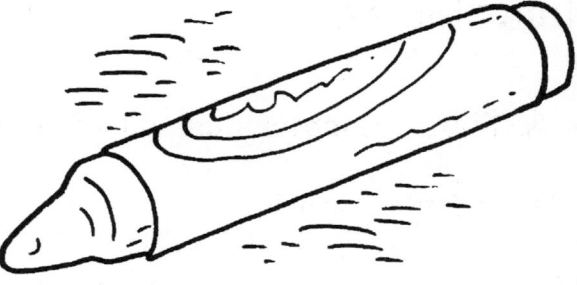

[ ]

[ ]

[ ]

- Decorate your labels, and bring them into school so that we can label your things.

To the helper:

- If your child is not sure about how to write his/her name, you could write the first label.
- Talk about the letters in their name; do they know what they are called, and what sound they make?

The letters in a child's name are the most important ones to them, as they are usually the first they learn. This activity will help children remember how to write their name, and to recognise it.

_____and
child

_____
helper(s)

_____

did this activity together

impact WRITING HOMEWORK

Spelling and phonics 19

To the helper:

- Talk together about what you think Martians look like; do they have legs, if so, how many? Once your child has drawn the picture, think about a name.
- *Invent* a spelling for the word. You will both need to listen to the sounds in the word, and then write them down. Tackle the words in sections, so that you can concentrate on the individual sounds, and let your child provide you with the letters to write down.

Inventing spellings is an important strategy for children to apply the rules and patterns they have learned about the English language.

_____ and

child

_____

helper(s)

did this activity together

20   **Spelling and phonics**

Mars landing

Imagine you have landed on Mars, and taken a photograph of a Martian.

- Draw your picture, and invent a Martian name.
- Write your Martian name under your picture.

impact WRITING HOMEWORK

Family album

- Who else apart from you is in your family?
- Draw a picture of each person in your family, and write down their name under each picture.
- Ask your helper to help you spell everyone's names.

To the helper:

- Talk about all your family; if there are a lot of you, suggest your child only draws the immediate family members!
- Give a hand with the writing, or spelling.

The letters in a child's name are the most important ones to them, as they are usually the first they learn. Names of family members are also important words; by writing them all down, the children will find it easier to recognise these names, and to write them.

_____and
child

_____
helper(s)

_____
did this activity together

impact WRITING HOMEWORK

Spelling and phonics

To the helper:

- Talk about the kind of rhyme together, that you might make up. Try to encourage your child to use more than just two rhyming words, eg 'A pig in a wig chewing a fig'.
- Talk together about the sound that is the rhyming part of your rhyme (eg **ig** in the rhyme above). Can your child think of any more words with that sound?

Recognising rhyming words is important in understanding spelling patterns in words, and will help with guessing the spellings of other words when children write on their own.

_____and

child

_____

helper(s)

_____

did this activity together

Spelling and phonics

Picture rhymes

- Make up a funny rhyme. It can be very short, for example: 'A pig in a wig', or 'A frog on a log'.

- Draw a picture of your rhyme.

- Write down your name next to your picture. Get your helper to write down your rhyme.

impact WRITING HOMEWORK

Unusual initial

When we think of a word to go with a letter, we often use 'apple' for the letter **A**.

- Can you think of a much more interesting and unusual thing that starts with the letter **A**?

- Write the letter and draw a picture to go with the word you have chosen.

To the helper:

- Talk together about all the things that start with the letter **A**.
- Help with the writing if necessary.

This activity gives the children experience in hunting for words that begin with specific letters. Learning initial sounds will help them when they are both reading and writing.

_____ and
child

_____
helper(s)

_____
did this activity together

Spelling and phonics

To the helper:

- Talk about all the animals you can think of which start with the same sound as your child's name; perhaps you can think of more than one! (You need only write down one.)
- Help with the writing if necessary.

The letters in a child's name are the most important ones to them, as they are usually the first they learn. This activity will help children remember how to write their name, and to recognise it. Learning initial sounds will help them when they are both reading and writing.

_____ and

child

_____

helper(s)

did this activity together

24 Spelling and phonics

Animal starter

● Think of an animal whose name starts with the same letter as your name.

For example:

M eena
M
o
n
k
e
y

S teve
n
a
k
e

impact WRITING HOMEWORK

Name rhyme

● Find a word that rhymes with your name, and make up a silly sentence that has both your name and the rhyming word in it.

For example: '**Rose** has ten **toes**', or '**Ben** likes to play in his **den**'.

To the helper:
● Thinking up the rhyme is the main task behind this activity, so you could write it down for your child.

Recognising rhyming words is important in understanding patterns in words, and might help with 'guessing' the spellings of other words when they are writing on their own.

_____ and
child

_____
helper(s)

_____
did this activity together

impact WRITING HOMEWORK

Spelling and phonics 25

To the helper:

- Talk about all the vehicles you can think of which start with the same sound as your child's name; perhaps you can think of more than one! (You need only write down one.)
- Help with the writing if necessary.

The letters in a child's name are the most important ones to them, as they are usually the first they learn. This activity will help children remember how to write their name, and to recognise it. Learning initial sounds will help them when they are both reading and writing.

_____and
child

_____
helper(s)

_____
did this activity together

26   Spelling and phonics

Vehicle starter

● Think of a vehicle whose name starts with the same letter as your name.

For example:
R afiq   C aroline
o   a
c   r
k
e
t

impact WRITING HOMEWORK

Alphabet choice

- Which is your favourite letter in the alphabet?
- Draw it big and decorate it.

n o p q r s t u v w x y z   a b c d e f g h i j k l m n o p q r s t u v w x y z a b c d e f g h i j k l m

---

To the helper:

- You will need to help your child say the alphabet. Which letters have sounds which your child likes? Which words begin with those letters? Perhaps the chosen letter is the initial of someone your child loves?

This activity helps children focus on the initial letters and the sounds they make. We are practising saying our alphabet and are talking about all the letters and the sounds they make.

_____ and
child

_____
helper(s)

_____
did this activity together

impact WRITING HOMEWORK

Spelling and phonics 27

To the helper:

- Help your child write down their letter. Run through the alphabet – your child may need quite a lot of help with this. Which three letters do come after their initial? How do you write those letters?

This activity helps children focus on the alphabet and the order of letters. It also helps them to remember how to form each letter correctly and to practise doing this.

_____and

child

_____

helper(s)

did this activity together

28   Spelling and phonics

Alphabet sequence

- Which letter starts your name?

- Write it down.

- Write down the three letters which come next in the alphabet.

impact WRITING HOMEWORK

Alphabet wheel

You will need counters and a dice to play this game.

● Take it in turns with your helper to throw the dice. Place your counter on the letter which starts your name. Throw the die and move round the track. When you land on a letter, you must say a word which begins with that letter. If you can think of a word you stay where you are. If not, you go back one space. Keep taking turns. Play until you get back to your own letter!

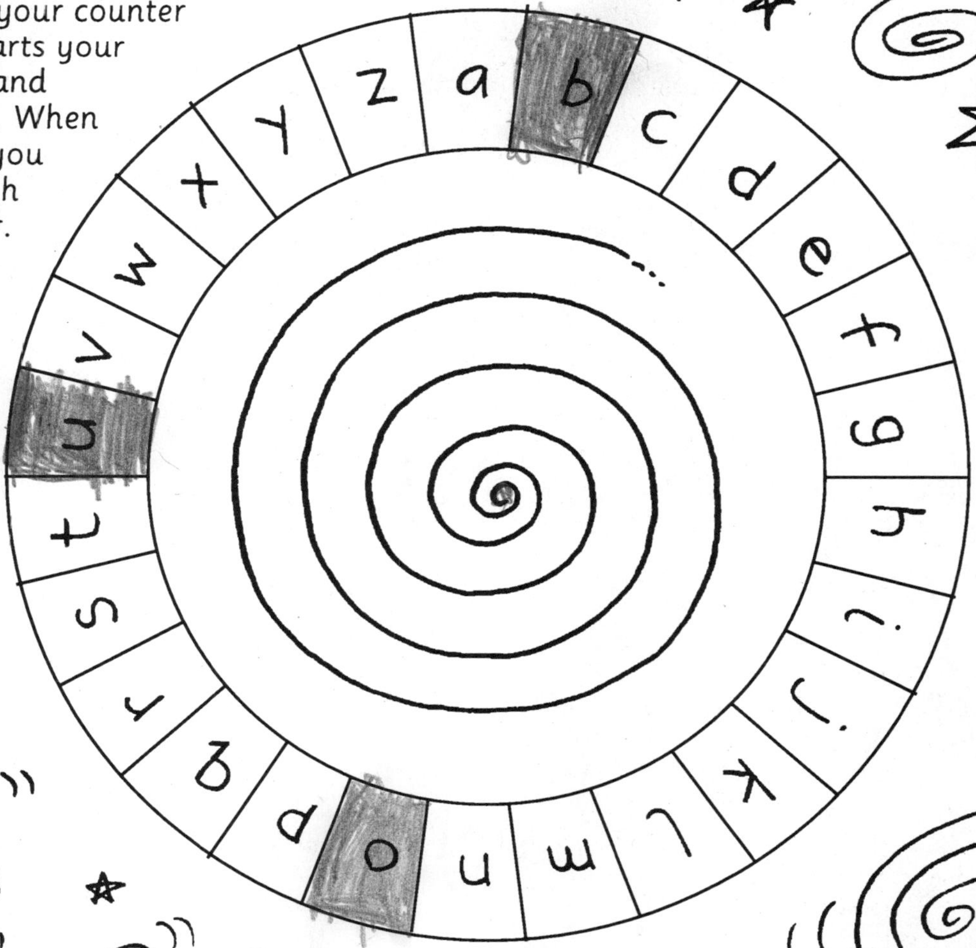

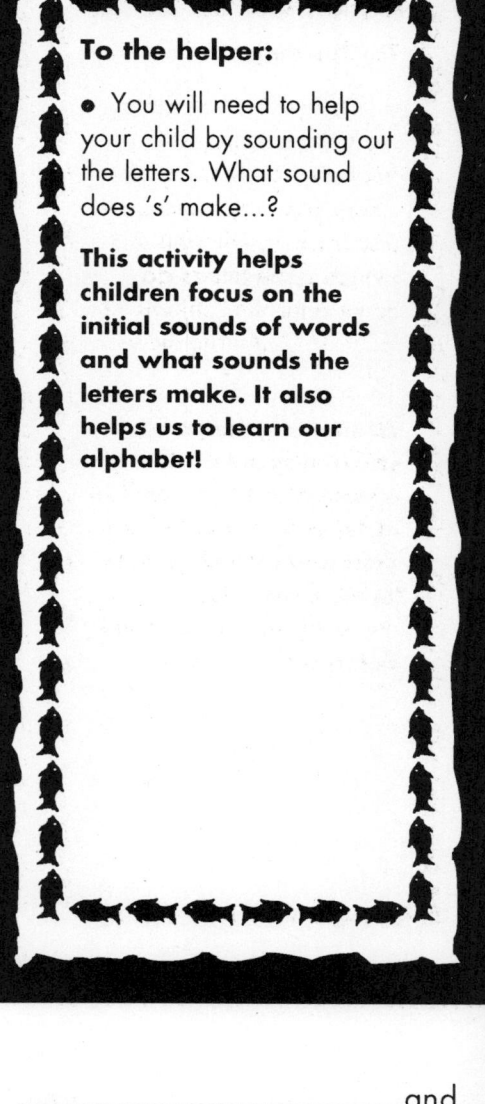

To the helper:

● You will need to help your child by sounding out the letters. What sound does 's' make...?

This activity helps children focus on the initial sounds of words and what sounds the letters make. It also helps us to learn our alphabet!

_____and
child

_____
helper(s)

_____

did this activity together

Spelling and phonics 29

To the helper:

- You will need to help by writing out the alphabet. Talk about the sounds the letters make. Which names begin with which sounds?

This activity helps children focus on the alphabet and the order of the letters. We are practising saying, and singing, our alphabet in class. We are also focusing on how each letter sounds.

_____and

child

_____

helper(s)

_____

did this activity together

Family and friends

- Write out the alphabet.

- Can you fill in the names of your family or close friends next to the letter which their names start with?

- Draw a picture of someone whose name you have filled in.

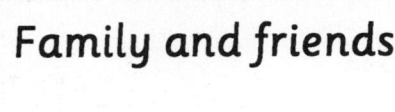

30 Spelling and phonics

impact WRITING HOMEWORK

Back to front!

- Choose a simple three-letter word. It should be an animal or an object. For example, cat.

- Now write it backwards! tac!

- What does this new animal or thing look like? Can you draw it?

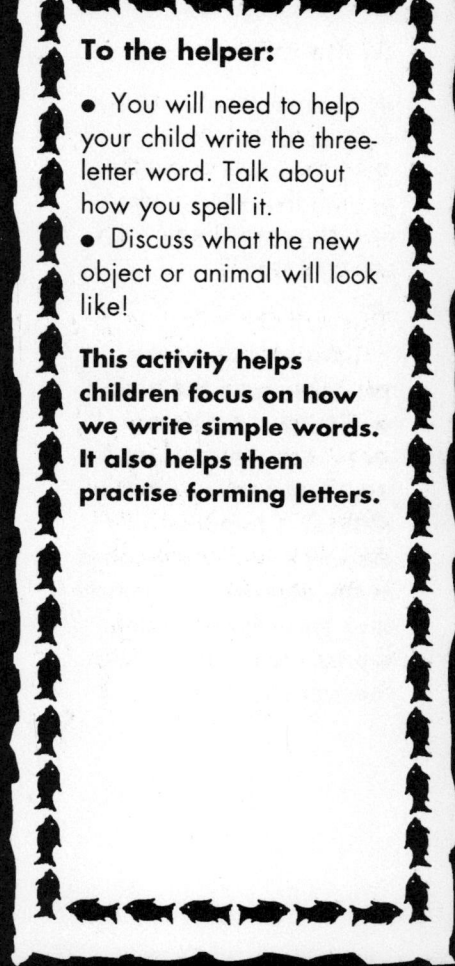

To the helper:
- You will need to help your child write the three-letter word. Talk about how you spell it.
- Discuss what the new object or animal will look like!

This activity helps children focus on how we write simple words. It also helps them practise forming letters.

_____ and
child

_____
helper(s)

_____
did this activity together

Spelling and phonics

To the helper:

- You may need to draw the actual letter for your child, and then help them to draw themselves around it! Perhaps they could be climbing the points of the **'M'** or clinging on to the stem of a **'T'**...

This activity will be used to help the children recognise their letters. We shall look at all the children's initials and discuss where they come in the alphabet. We shall also talk about other words which begin with the same sound.

_____and

child

_____

helper(s)

_____

did this activity together

Letter portrait

● Draw a picture of yourself with the letter which starts your name.

So, if your name is **'Mary'**, you will make the letter **'M'** part of your picture.

Opposite ends

- Can you think of a word which begins with 'a'?
- Can you think of a word which begins with 'z'?
- Write them both down.

- Do you know that **a** is the first letter and **z** is the last letter of the alphabet. Try saying your alphabet with your helper. How far can you get?

- Write down one letter which comes somewhere in between **a** and **z** and think of a word which begins with it!

To the helper:

- You will probably need to help your child say the alphabet. Try to make it a sort of song by saying it in a rhythmic way – or you can actually sing it! Help choose a letter and a word to go with it.

This activity helps children learn the alphabet. We shall look at all the words the children bring in, and discuss the initial letters. We shall also be practising saying our alphabet together!

_____ and
child

_____
helper(s)

_____
did this activity together

impact WRITING HOMEWORK

Spelling and phonics 33

To the helper:

- You may need to give quite a lot of help with this activity. Talk about words like 'it', 'on' and 'in'. Give one or two examples and see if your child can guess another one. Make the list together, to include all those you and your child can come up with.

This activity is an early spelling activity. It helps the children to think about how we write certain words, and how the sounds match the written letters. Many of these words are also very commonly used and useful to know!

_____ and

child

_____

helper(s)

_____

did this activity together

Only two!

Some words have only two letters!

- Can you and your helper think of any words like this?
- Write a list of as many as you can think of.

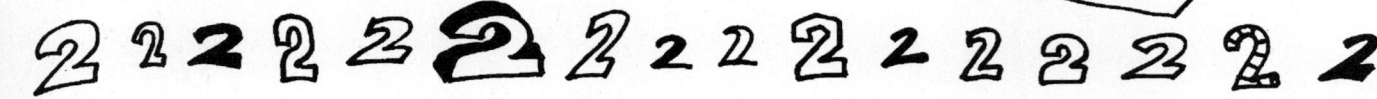

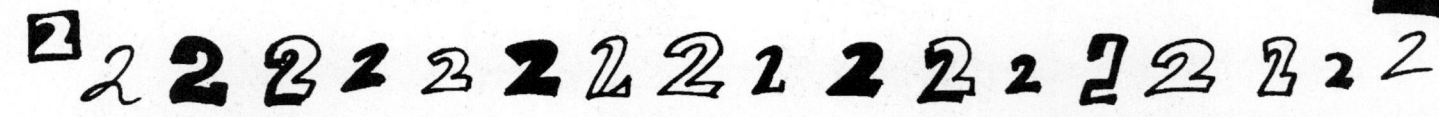

Spelling and phonics

impact WRITING HOMEWORK

Y words

- Can you think of three words which end in the letter 'y'?
- With your helper, write them down.
- Draw a picture to go with one of your words.

To the helper:
- Talk about what sound the **'y'** at the end of a word makes. Give the child a couple of examples, for example smelly! yucky! Talk about all the words they can think of before choosing three to write down.

This activity focuses the children's minds on how words are written, and how we can remember how to spell them. Initial sounds are very helpful, but so are endings. This activity helps children to recognise sound-letter patterns.

_____ and
child

_____
helper(s)

_____
did this activity together

impact WRITING HOMEWORK   **Spelling and phonics**   35

To the helper:

● Write your street name clearly using a capital letter to start, then small letters. Talk about how you write it and how it sounds. How many letters has the name got?

This activity helps us to think about initial sounds and how we write words. We shall categorise the various street names according to their first letter and also how many letters they have.

_____ and
child

_____
helper(s)

did this activity together

Street names

● What is the name of your street?

● Ask your helper to write it down.

● What letter does it begin with?

● What letter does it end in?

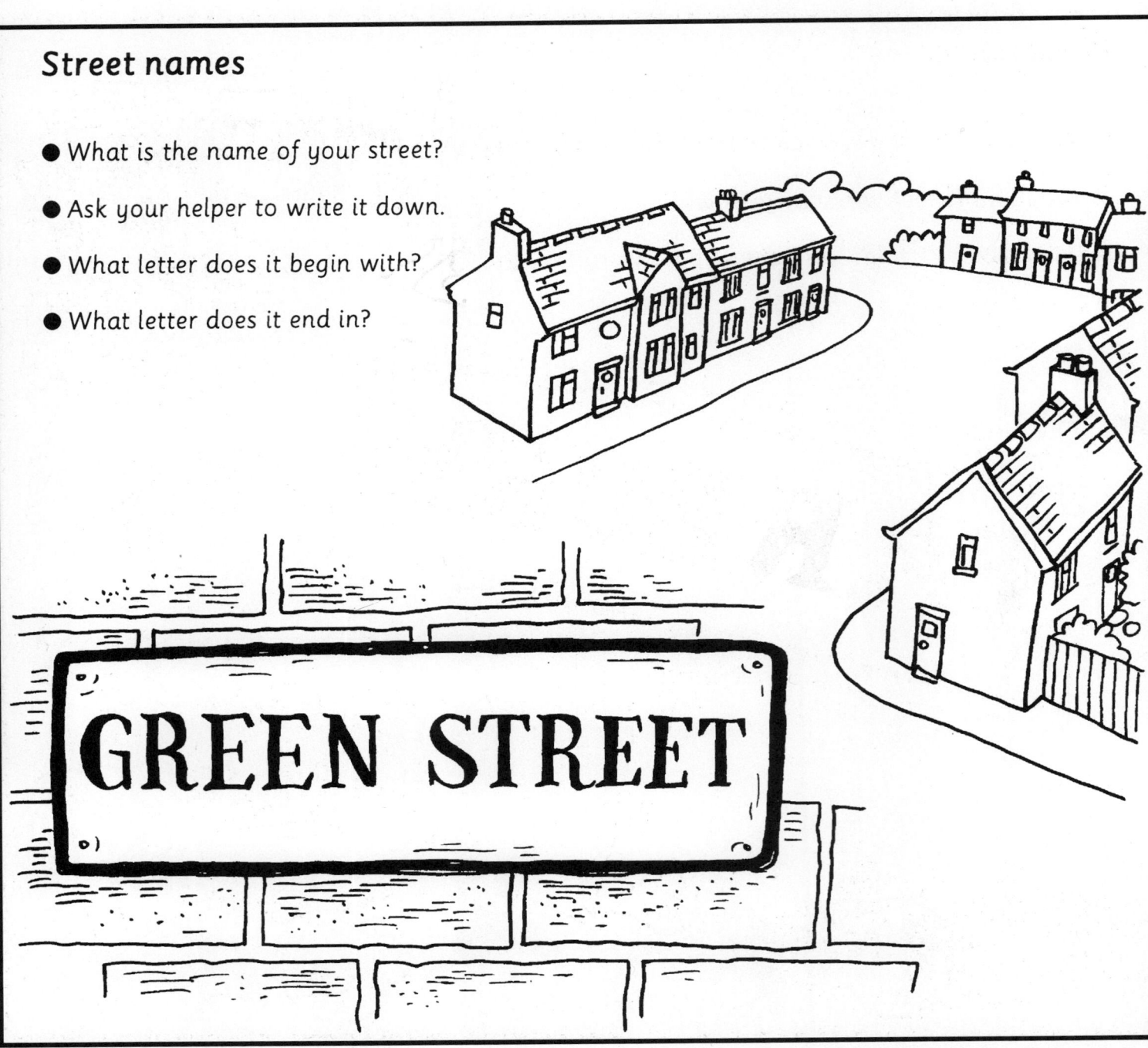

36 **Spelling and phonics**

impact WRITING HOMEWORK

Place names

- What is the name of the place where you live?
- Ask your helper to write it down.
- What letter does it begin with?
- What letter does it end in?

To the helper:

- Write the name of your village, town or area clearly using a capital letter to start and then small letters. Discuss how you write it and how it sounds. How many letters has the name got? If the place is mentioned in the school name, can your child recognise the word from a school sweatshirt or school newsletter?

This activity helps us to think about initial sounds and how we write words. We shall be practising writing our addresses, and learning how to spell the necessary words.

_____and
child

_____
helper(s)

_____
did this activity together

impact WRITING HOMEWORK

Spelling and phonics 37

To the helper:

- Talk about the pet. What type of animal is it? Does its name suggest what animal it is? Talk to your child about how you write the name – its initial sound and so on.

This activity helps us to think about initial sounds and how we write words. We shall categorise the various pet names according to their first letter. We shall also talk about what the names suggest, and how appropriate they are.

_____and

child

_____

helper(s)

did this activity together

38   **Spelling and phonics**

Pet names

- Have you got a pet or do you know someone with a pet?

- What is the pet's name? What letter does it begin with?

- Ask someone to write it down.

- Draw a picture of the pet.

impact WRITING HOMEWORK

Teddy names

- Have you got a favourite teddy or soft toy?

- What is his or her name? What letter does it begin with? Write down the name.

- Now draw a picture of your teddy.

To the helper:
- Write the teddy's name clearly using small letters. Talk about how you write it and how it sounds. Discuss how teddy got his/her name.

This activity helps us to think about initial sounds and how we write words. We shall categorise the various teddy's names according to their first letter and also how many letters they have. We shall also discuss how the teddy bears got their names and what they say about their characters!

_____ and
child

_____
helper(s)

_____
did this activity together

impact WRITING HOMEWORK

Spelling and phonics   39

To the helper:

- Talk about the animals your child particularly likes. For example, they might choose a cat. What sound does the cat make; could it be 'meeeaoouw' or 'pssssst'.
- Talk about the sound and say it slowly, so your child has a chance to work out the individual sounds of letters in the word. Remember there is no correct way to spell these sounds, the children are making them up.

Inventing spellings is an important strategy for children to apply the rules and patterns they have learned about the English language.

_____and

child

_____

helper(s)

_____

did this activity together

Animal magic

- What is your favourite animal?
- Draw a picture of it with a speech bubble coming out of its mouth.

- What sound does your animal make?
- Try and write down the sound using the letters you know in the speech bubble.

40   Spelling and phonics   *impact* WRITING HOMEWORK

Messy me

- Think of a word to describe yourself.

  It must begin with the same letter as your name.

- Ask your helper to write it down for you.

- Draw a picture.

To the helper:

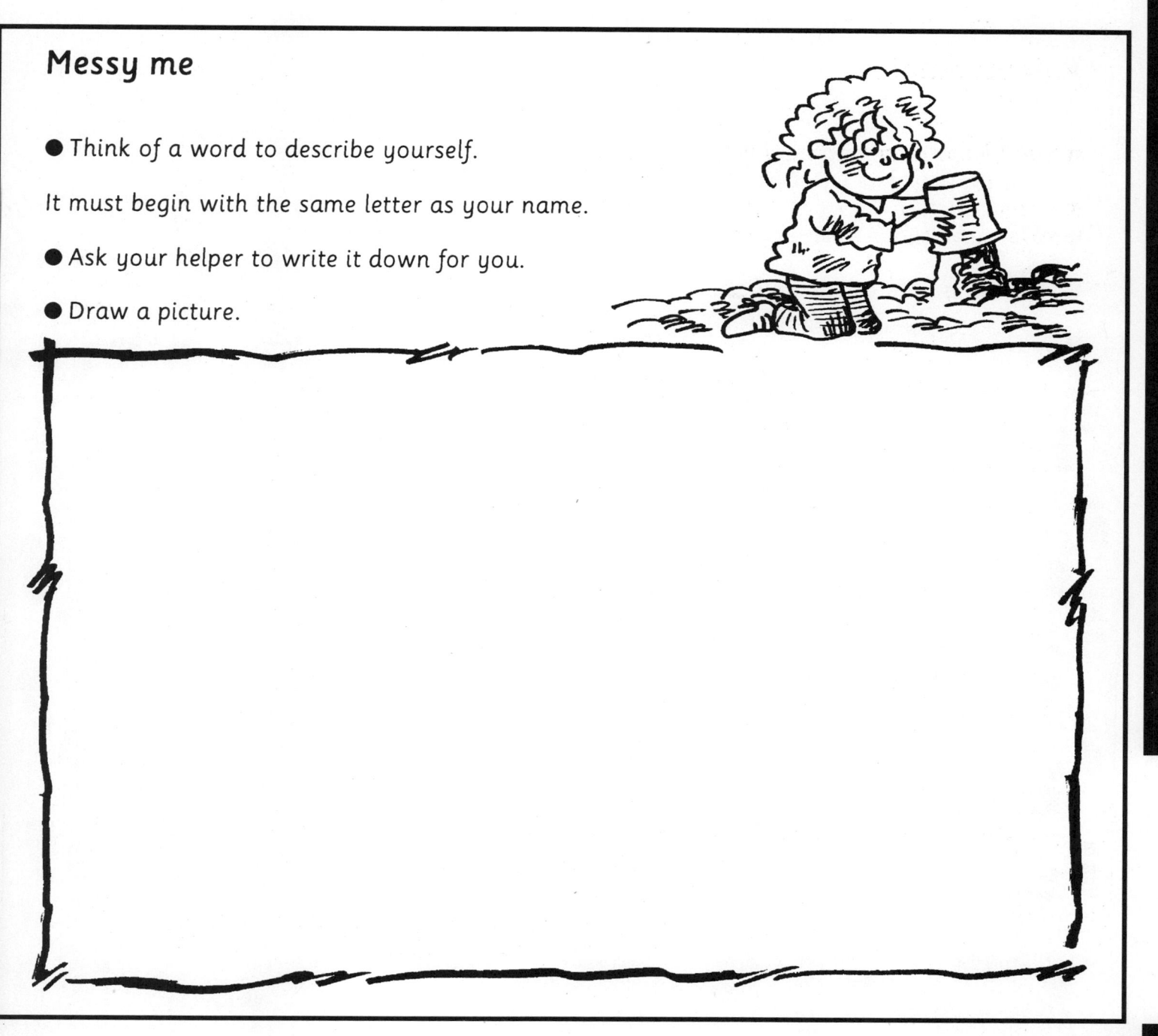

- You will need to help your child by writing down their initial. Which words can they think of which begin with the same sound? Help them by writing down their chosen word next to their name.

This activity helps children recognise initial letters and the sounds they make. We shall categorise all the 'describing' words which they bring in and discuss what they mean.

_____ and
child

_____
helper(s)

_____
did this activity together

impact WRITING HOMEWORK

Spelling and phonics   41

To the helper:

● You will need to help your child by talking about the sound their initial makes and then suggesting some 'doing' words to give them the general idea. For example, running, climbing, fishing...

This activity alerts the children to the sounds that letters make. It also helps us to start sorting words according to their function – for example, doing words and names.

_____and

child

_____

helper(s)

_____

did this activity together

42   Spelling and phonics

Wilf walking

● Can you think of anything you might be doing which starts with the same letter as your name?

● Write down your name.

● Write what you are doing beside it.

● Draw a picture.

impact WRITING HOMEWORK

Which letter?

- Look at the letter which starts your name.
- Write it down.
- Where in the alphabet does it come?

For example, **Rose** – **'R'** is the 18th letter.
Hannah – **'H'** is the 8th letter.

To the helper:

- You will probably need to help your child say the alphabet. Try to make it a sort of song by saying it in a rhythmic way – or you can actually sing it! Talk about which letter is their initial, and count through the alphabet to find it. It may help to write out the alphabet.

This activity helps children learn the alphabet. We shall look at all their initials, and discuss the sounds they make. We shall count and work out which is first, second and so on. We shall also be practising saying our alphabet.

_____ and
child

_____
helper(s)

_____
did this activity together

impact WRITING HOMEWORK

Spelling and phonics 43

To the helper:

- You will probably need to help your child say their name as a series of beats. Write it down as you say it, with the same breaks.

This activity supports and reinforces children's learning to write their own name. It also helps us to focus on the structure of words – how the number of syllables helps us know how to spell them.

_____ and
child

_____
helper(s)

did this activity together

44   Spelling and phonics

Drum beats

- How many drum beats in your name?

For example
Man-deep   Tim   Har-ri-et
bang-bang   bang   bang-bang-bang

- Ask someone to help you clap your name.

- Write your name and write the number of beats too.

impact WRITING HOMEWORK

Initial names

- What letter does your name begin with? Can you think of any other names which start with the same letter?

- Write a list.

- Which name do you like best?

To the helper:

- You will probably need to help by suggesting a few names. Talk about which are boy's names and which are girl's names. Write the list with your child, talking about how you write the different names. You only need two or three!

This activity helps children learn to think about their initial letters and the sounds they make. We shall categorise the names under the different letters of the alphabet and also practise saying our alphabet!

_____and
child

_____
helper(s)

_____

did this activity together

impact WRITING HOMEWORK

Spelling and phonics 45

To the helper:

● You will probably need to help your child say the alphabet. Try to make it a sort of song by saying it in a rhythmic way – or you can actually sing it!

This activity helps children to learn the alphabet. We shall look at all the words the children bring in, and discuss their initial letters and the sounds they make. We shall also be practising saying our alphabet!

_____and

child

_____

helper(s)

did this activity together

46 **Spelling and phonics**

Beginning and end

● Write down the first letter of your name.

● Write down the last letter.

● Think of something which begins with each letter and draw two pictures.

● Write the names of the things that you have drawn.

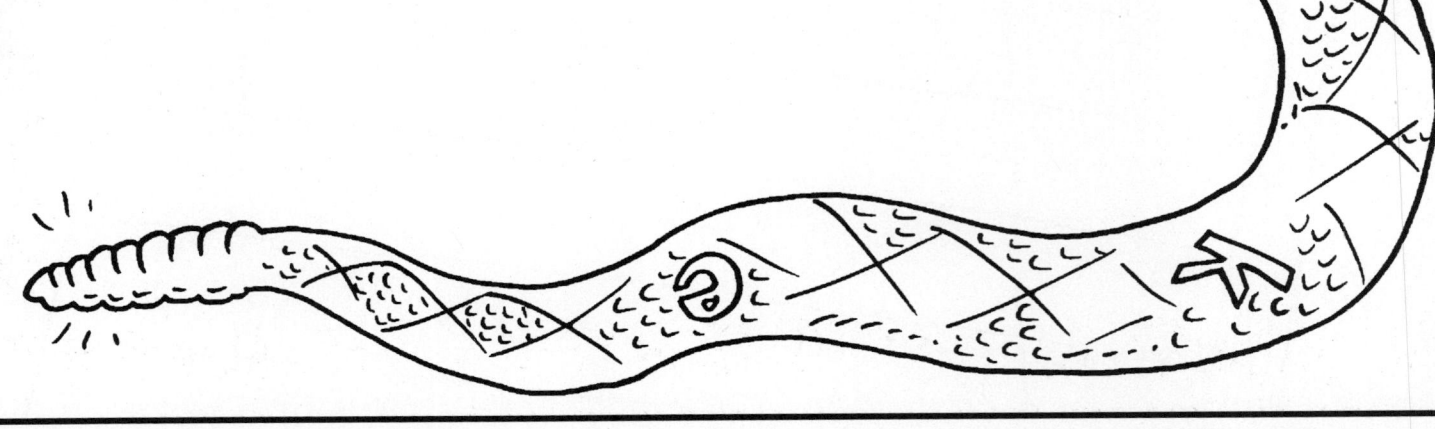

impact WRITING HOMEWORK

But I'm not tired...

- What excuses do you find for not going to bed on time?
- With your helper write down one excuse!

It must begin with 'But...'

Remember to leave spaces between the words.

But...

To the helper:

- Let your child think of an excuse and then help write it down. Talk about how you write the words and how we leave spaces between each word.

This activity helps children compose a simple sentence. We are looking in school at how starting words like 'but' and 'when' are spelled.

_____and
child

_____
helper(s)

_____
did this activity together

impact WRITING HOMEWORK

Spelling and phonics 47

To the helper:

- Help your child write down the character's name. Talk about the first letter of the name. Can they think of other words which begin with that letter?

This activity helps children focus on the initial letters and the sounds they make. We shall look at all the names which the children bring in and we shall be practising saying our alphabet!

_____ and

child

_____

helper(s)

_____

did this activity together

48   **Spelling and phonics**

Cartoon character

- Who is your favourite cartoon character?

- Write down the name of your character.

- What is the first letter of the name?

impact WRITING HOMEWORK

Teachers' Notes
YEAR ONE

Word use Collect all the 'sea' words. Make a 'backwards' book with cutaway pages so that the word 'sea' is visible on each page. Look for 'sea' words when you are reading with the children. Differentiate between 'ce', 'see', and 'sea' words. Look at how they are spelled differently even though they sound the same. Can the children find any other words that sound the same but are spelled differently? (To, two, too etc.)

Peng-aroo Display the children's ridiculous animals; whose is the funniest? Read 'Tog the Dog' with them. Talk about real animal combinations eg asses, breeds of dog. Design a new fruit that is a combination of two of your favourites – what will its name be? How will you spell it? Talk about the importance of 'having a go' and using the knowledge that they already have about sounds and letters.
Tog the Dog; Colin and Jacqui Hawkins (Picture Puffin).

Rhyme detective Use this sheet to write in a word before you hand out this activity. Re-use the original for different words. Collect all the rhyming words together. Are there any with the same endings? Is there a pattern? Sort the words into groups of matching endings. What are the exceptions? Try and learn the most common ending. Write down the beginnings of words for children and let them finish the word.

Letter search Fill in a letter on this sheet before you send it home. Re-use the sheet for different letters. Write a selection of the rhyming words on a large sheet of paper, or on to a board all the children can see. Use three different coloured pens – one where the letter is the initial letter, one where it's in the middle, and one where it's at the end of the word. Ask the children to come up and underline a few words each with the special pens. If the children have been identifying the letter 's' ask: what does it mean (usually) if s is at the end of a word? How does it change the word? (Plurals) Practise writing plural versions of words. Write the singular down in say, a blue pen; and the children can make them into plurals by adding an s with a red pen.

Cereal word hunt Make a list of the words that the children found. Write out the alphabet, and make a cereal-word alphabet frieze. Discuss which words are common and which are rare. Can the children design a cereal-packet for themselves. What will they call their new cereal? What will it taste like? What words will they use to describe it?

Alphabet animals Make an animals alphabet frieze to go around the classroom. Share out the letters amongst the children and ask them to paint a picture to display next to a large, colourful letter (you could provide templates, or outlines of the letters). Write down the names of the animals next to the pictures. Read through the alphabet frieze with the children drawing attention to the shapes of all the letters.

'Cr'/'St'/'Fl' hunt Collect all the words that the children have found. Has anyone thought of words with the sound in the middle? Write a silly structure using the children's ideas and some relevant adjectives (i.e. crazy/animal/crunchy; sticky/stumped/stodgy; floppy/flowery/flappy). The children can then illustrate their own sentences.

Baby talk Is there anyone in the class who still answers to a 'baby' or pet name? Talk about how the children have written down the words. Since they are not real words, the children will have had to invent spellings for them. Talk to the children about how they decided on the letters they used – what knowledge have they drawn on to produce these words? Emphasise how wonderful their attempts are, and talk about the importance of 'having a go' themselves when they write.

Last name animals Make an animals alphabet frieze to go around the classroom. Share out the letters to each child so they can paint a picture of their animal next to a large, colourful letter (you may want to provide a template, or an outline of the letter so it is clear for all the children to read). Choose unusual animals to go with each letter. Write down the names of the animals next to the pictures.

Moving letters Get the children to share their ideas. Display the pictures with appropriate labels; for example 'Rebecca's rocket', or 'Helen's helicopter' etc. Read the labels with the children. Talk about apostrophe s ('s) and what it means. Can you sort them into alphabetical order? Which letters of the alphabet are missing?

Sound sums How many different words have the children found? Talk about the meanings of the words. Perhaps the children can write some definitions of some of their words or illustrate their meaning by drawing pictures. Make a class book of some of the more interesting words and definitions of words and their illustrations. Talk about other sound sums – e.g. st-ack, st-ar, st-air etc.

Alphabet vehicles Paint large pictures in school and make a vehicles alphabet frieze to go around the classroom. Write down the name of the vehicle next to each picture.

Fat cat and small ball Look at everyone's pictures together; if they are clear enough, you could just read half the rhyme, and see if the children can guess the end. For example; 'A big — and a —'. Write the rhymes up on the board. Talk about how (most) of the rhymes have 'matching' endings e.g. -ig, -ot, -og, etc. Prepare some pictures like the children's and write the rhyme next to each picture. Get the children to underline the part that rhymes each time.

Number rhymes Put together some class number rhymes made up of collections of the best lines which the children brought in. Write these out on a large piece of paper and encourage the children to illustrate each line. Make some books of the rhymes and illustrate each page. Perhaps the books can be lent to the nursery or reception classes to help the younger children learn to count. Extend the activity by encouraging the children to make rhymes for all the numbers up to ten.

Animal names Make a large animal alphabet frieze in class. Ask the children to paint their animals on large pieces of paper to make the frieze bright and colourful. Talk about which of the animals live on land, which live in water. Are any of them birds? Classify them. Discuss their size. Which is the largest animal on the alphabet frieze? Which is the smallest?

Days of the week The children can make a zig-zag book of the days of the week. They can then take it home and draw a picture of something that they do each evening. Alternatively, you can make a large class zig-zag book of all the days in the week and include drawings by each child of the activity the chose for their favourite day.

Body parts Draw a large figure of a child on the wall and allow the children to write one label each and place it in the appropriate place! Write a list of all the body parts and cut up the word into strips. Place the strips in a cloth bag, and ask a child to take one out and to place it on the figure. Play in two

impact WRITING HOMEWORK

Spelling and phonics 49

teams, taking it in turns to go and see which team recognises and can place the most words!

Address labels Let the children write their addresses in a class 'address book'. Perhaps they can each illustrate their entry with a picture of their home. Write the address of one of the children on the board. Talk about the various parts of the address – the name, the surname, the number of the road, the town and county and the post-code. Discuss the variations, e.g. some houses have names. Talk about the different names for 'road', e.g. street, avenue, crescent, etc.

Mixed numbers Write up the numbers on the board without their vowels and fill them in. Let the children work in five groups finding three or four letter words which have one of the vowels as their heart – one group can work on 'a' words, another can work on 'e' words, and so on.

Emotional sounds Make a list of 'happy' sounds, 'sad' sounds, 'angry' sounds and 'scared' sounds. Now make a poster of happy words (glad, laughing, funny etc.), another poster of sad words (down-hearted, weepy, depressed, unhappy, boo-hoo...), another of angry words (cross, annoyed, bad-tempered, No, no, NO!...), and another of scared words (frightened, terrified, creepy, spooky...). Talk about how we write these words. Draw the children's attention to the sounds in the words. Are they the same as the sounds they brought in from home?

Greetings/Fare-thee-well Let the children share all their words. Teach the children how to say hello and goodbye in as many languages as you can, drawing upon the knowledge of the children in the class. Make a 'hello' poster and a 'goodbye' poster with as many different words in as many different languages – ancient and modern – as possible.

End of the line Make some lists of different word endings; -ion, -ing, -ed, -er, -st etc. How many endings have the children managed to find. Let the children work in groups with one of the more common endings each. See how many words they can find with that ending, and then put their words in alphabetical order.

Gift tags The children can make gift tags in class for each other, and then draw a picture of the gift they would like to put in the imaginary parcel. Be creative e.g. one child might give another a suit that makes him invisible, or a pair of shoes that can make you fly through the air, or a magic potion that turns you into a cat for a night! They can write a few words about their gift and what magical properties it has.

Abracadabra! Let each child write the magic word they have invented on a piece of paper – cut it out into the shape of a 'splash!' and mount it on brightly coloured paper. They can each draw a picture of something that happens when their magic word is spoken. Mount the children's drawing in a circle around a large paper wand.

Illuminated letters The children can make a complete alphabet frieze consisting of illuminated letters. Think of things beginning with each letter to decorate them. Talk about the decorations that the monks used – e.g. serpents for 's' and dragons for 'd'. Discuss the use of mythical beasts – winged horses and half-horse, half-man, mermaids etc.

Turn about The children can play this game again in class. Pin up an alphabet frieze. Sit in a circle (large group/whole class) and start with 'a'. The first child has to think of a word beginning with 'a'. If he/she succeeds they may take a multilink cube! The next child has to think of a word beginning with 'b' and, if they succeed, can take a cube. Keep going around the circle. When you get to the end of the alphabet, see how many cubes each child has.

Alphabet names Make a class alphabet of names. Talk about names from other countries and cultures. Discuss the way in which some names recur across culture and language. E.g. Mary, Marie, Maria, Mari... John, Jean, Ian... Discuss the origin of as many of the names as you can. Do the children know where their name came from, what it means or even why their parents chose it?

Coded alphabet Write a few words in code and let the children try to work out what they say. Talk about the children's codes. They can swap names and swap coded messages, and try to work out each other's. Practise writing the alphabet in this way. Explain that the vowels are in a list down the side of the page. Talk about how almost all words have one of these five letters.

Code names The children can write out names in code, and those of one or two people in their family. Display the whole alphabet and the codes. The children can then use a calculator to help them work out how much their name is worth by adding up all the codes. Whose name is worth the most? Whose name is worth the least? Is the name with the most letters worth the most?

Secret names The children should write out their complete names – i.e. first names and surnames. They can then decorate the piece of paper with their name on it. Then they can each write out their name in the 'secret' way and decorate that. Make a display of the real names and the secret names muddled up. Talk about which name goes with which secret name!

Backwards names! Talk about which letter the children's names begin with and which letter they end with. Can you make a class alphabet using either the names back to front or the names the right way round? Are there any letters in the alphabet which get left out completely? Make an 'upside-down' class book of all the pictures of the children turned upside down. Let them draw their teacher upside-down at the front!

Common words Use the children's lists to make some large class posters with common words on them. Write out the twenty or so most common words on small cards, place all the cards into a cloth bag. Divide the group into two teams. Take it in turns to take out a card. The child who takes it out shows it to his/her team, and they must agree what word it is. If they are right they take a multilink cube. The winner are the first team to collect ten multilink.

Newspaper alphabet Make a class alphabet frieze using newspaper letters. Let the children look at some newspaper headlines and cut out some common words. Make a list of the most common words to help children learn them. Can the children write their own headlines for a story about something that happened to them!

Three letter guess Play the same game in class, either on the rug with the teacher or one or two children choosing a word and allowing the rest of the children to guess it, or in small groups. Extend the game for some of the children by allowing them to choose four letter words. They must be able to spell any words they choose! Another extension of this game is playing the game 'hangman'.

Station names Pin up the names of the stations on the walls and encourage the children to draw a picture of themselves with their name beside it. Their picture can then go nearest to the appropriate station. Try the game with other words, like animals or vehicles. Draw pictures of animals or vehicles, label them neatly and place them near the appropriate station.

Word use

● How many words or phrases can you and other people in your house think up which begin with **sea**...

For example, **Sea**l
              Sea-green

● Write down a list of them.

To the helper:

● You can use any words that begin with the three letters **sea**.
● Help your child with the writing if the list gets too long, or they get tired.

Writing lists is an important skill, as a quick way of collecting and sorting ideas. This activity also develops children's ability to construct letter strings found in longer words. We shall share all our *sea* words back in the classroom.

_____and
child

_____
helper(s)

_____
did this activity together

Impact WRITING HOMEWORK

Spelling and phonics   51

To the helper:

- Take it in turns to think of ridiculous combinations, and talk about what they would look like.
- Give a hand with the spelling, or sounds if you need to.

This activity is about having fun with words. Children naturally enjoy playing with words, and this gives them a reason to write them down. We shall all share our strange animals at school, and use them to write stories in the classroom.

_____and
child

_____
helper(s)

_____
did this activity together

Peng-aroo

Something strange has happened at the zoo! All the animals names are muddled up!

● Can you make up an animal name, like this –

Kanga-guin

Oster-ake

● Draw a picture of your muddled up animal and write its name down!

52 Spelling and phonics

impact WRITING HOMEWORK

Rhyme detective

- Be a rhyme detective – hunt for words that rhyme with _____
- How many can you find?
- Write down as many as you can.
- Can your helper find any more?

To the helper:

- Talk about this sound that you are looking for; let your child come up with a few rhyming words (they do not have to be spelled the same, they just have to rhyme), and then you could suggest any more that you can think of.
- Take over with the writing if the list gets rather long.

Recognising rhyming words is an important part of understanding spelling patterns in words, and will help with guessing the spellings of other words when the children are writing on their own.

_____ and

child

_____

helper(s)

did this activity together

Spelling and phonics

To the helper:

- This activity has two themes: choosing a favourite page and finding a particular letter.
- First, talk about your child's choice of page, as well as the whole book. Did they choose because of the storyline, characters, or illustrations?
- Look for words with __ in them – you may count words that have __ at the beginning, middle or end of the word.
- You may need to help your child where the __ is in the middle of the word.

Finding a specific letter on a page focuses attention on the letters that constitute words.

_____ and

child

_____

helper(s)

did this activity together

54   Spelling and phonics

Letter search

- Find your favourite page in your book with writing on.
- How many words with __h__ in them can you find?
- Write one of them down.

impact WRITING HOMEWORK

Cereal word hunt

- What are the first three letters of your name?
- Write them down.
- Choose one of those letters.
- How many words can you find on your cereal packet that begin with that letter?

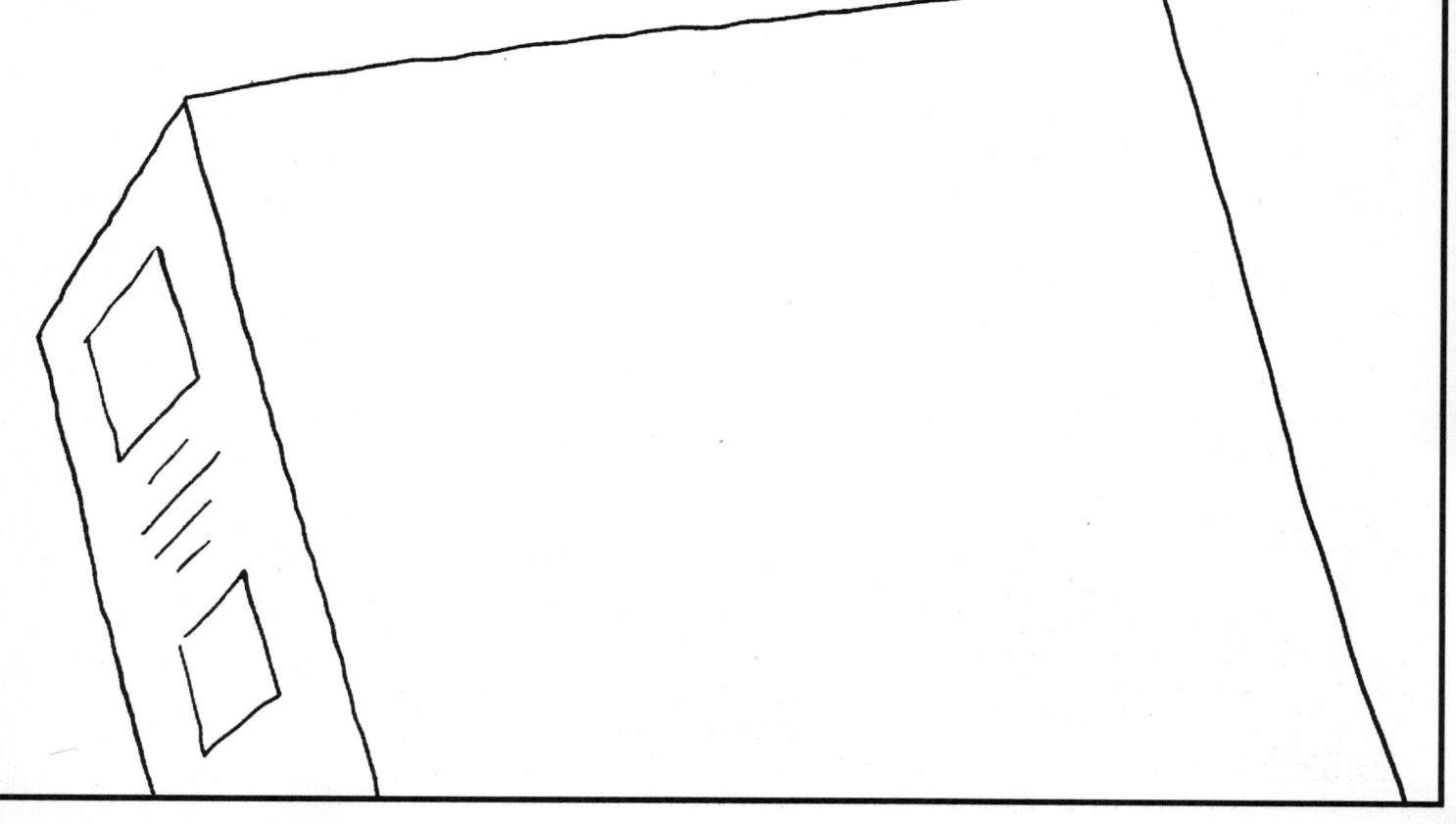

To the helper:
- Talk about the letters in your child's name; can he/she name all of them?
- Look at the cereal box you have chosen, and hunt for words of the same initial letter (for example, if your child's name is **Peter**, look for all the words on the box that begin with **P** first, and then **e** and so on).
- Your child may want you to write down the words you find.

The first letters in a child's name are generally the first ones they learn, and so become very important to them. Finding other things that start with those letters draws on their interest in them.

_____ and
child

_____
helper(s)

_____
did this activity together

impact WRITING HOMEWORK

Spelling and phonics

To the helper:

- Write down the alphabet first, leaving a space by each letter big enough for a picture.
- Start with the letters for which your child can think of an animal easily.
- Do not worry if you cannot think of an animal for each letter; try asking other people for help when you run out of ideas.

Listing words in alphabetical order is a useful dictionary skill. By having to think of an animal for each letter they are having to use their knowledge of the alphabet, which is an important precursor to understanding how to use a dictionary.

_____and

child

_____

helper(s)

_____

did this activity together

Spelling and phonics

Alphabet animals

● Can you think of an animal for each letter of the alphabet?

For example, you could have **lizard** for l or a **tarantula** for **t**, etc.

● Write down the letters, then draw pictures of the animals, next to the letters.

impact WRITING HOMEWORK

'Cr' hunt

- How many things starting with **'cr'** can you find in the room where you might find some **crisps**?

- Write down at least three things.

Your helper could help you write down any others that you find.

To the helper:

- Start off by talking about **'cr'** words, so that your child has a clear idea of the sound.
- Then look around the house for **'cr'** things.
- If you found a lot of things, your child could write down the first three (help with spelling) and then after that you could write down the words *together*. For example, your child writes down the **'cr'** each time, and you fill in the rest of the world.

This activity will help reinforce the sound cr. Recognising and being able to use simple and commonly used prefixes is an important stage in developing spelling skills.

_____and
child

_____
helper(s)

_____

did this activity together

impact WRITING HOMEWORK

Spelling and phonics

To the helper:

- Start by talking about **'st'** words so that your child has a clear idea of the sound.
- Then look around the house for **'st'** things.
- If you found a lot of things, your child could write down the first three (help with spelling) and then you could write down the words *together*, for example, your child writes down the **'st'** each time, and you fill in the rest of the word.

This activity helps reinforce the sound 'st'. Recognising and being able to use simple and commonly used prefixes is an important stage in developing spelling skills.

_____ and

child

_____

helper(s)

_____

did this activity together

58   Spelling and phonics

'St' hunt

- How many **'st'** things can you find up**st**airs?

- Write down at least 3 things.

Your helper could write down any others that you find.

impact WRITING HOMEWORK

'Fl' hunt

● How many things starting with '**fl**' can you find on or near the **floor**?

● Write down at least three things.

Your helper could help you write down any others that you find.

To the helper:

- Start off by talking about **'fl'** words so that your child has a clear idea of the sound.
- Then look around the house for **'fl'** things.
- If you found a lot of things, your child could write down the first three (help with spelling) and then after that you could write down the words *together* eg. your child writes down the **'fl'** each time, and you fill in the rest of the word.

This activity will help reinforce the sound 'fl'. Recognising and being able to use simple and commonly used prefixes is an important stage in developing spelling skills.

_____and

child

_____

helper(s)

_____

did this activity together

Spelling and phonics

To the helper:

- You are probably going to have to *invent* a spelling for your word, since it is a mispronunciation. To do this, you will have to listen to the sounds in the word, and then write them down. Tackle the words in sections, so you can focus on the individual sounds, and let your child provide the letters to write down.

Inventing spellings is an important strategy for children to apply the rules and patterns they have learned about the English language. It also reinforces the relationship between sound and symbol – how a word sounds and how we write it down.

_____ and

child

_____

helper(s)

did this activity together

Baby talk

- When you were little, were there any words that you could not say very well? Ask someone who knew you well when you were learning to talk.

- Write down how you used to say the word, and then next to it how it should be spelled.

- Try to think of at least five words. If you cannot think of any, then ask someone at home if they remember any that they had trouble learning when they were learning to speak.

(For example: **'Chrisfa'** – Christopher)

Spelling and phonics

impact WRITING HOMEWORK

Last name animals

- Write down your surname (your last name).
- Look at all the letters, and draw a picture of an animal to go with each one.

To the helper:

- Help your child write down their surname clearly. Talk about what animal goes with each letter.

This activity helps children to focus on the initial sounds by asking them to sound out the names of all the animals they have to draw. It also makes sure they know how to write their surname!

_____and
child

_____
helper(s)

_____
did this activity together

impact WRITING HOMEWORK

Spelling and phonics 61

To the helper:

● This activity helps the child with initial sounds. Make the *sound* of each letter to help them think of a vehicle to draw.

We are constantly drawing the children's attention to the sounds that individual letters make, and also to the sounds made by pairs of letters, eg. ch, th and st. This activity is part of this process.

_____and

child

_____

helper(s)

did this activity together

62 **Spelling and phonics**

Moving letters

● Write down your first name.

● Look at each letter, and draw a picture of a vehicle to go with each one.

impact WRITING HOMEWORK

Sound sums

Some words are built using smaller parts, and adding them together.

For example, **'black'** is built from **'bl'** and **'ack'**.

● Can you find any other parts that will go with **'bl'** to make new words?

To the helper:

● Help your child, perhaps by suggesting a couple of words to get them started! For example, blue... blood...

We are encouraging the children to think about how words are constructed. This helps them in their progress to becoming independent writers.

_____and

child

_____

helper(s)

_____

did this activity together

impact WRITING HOMEWORK

Spelling and phonics 63

To the helper:

- Write out the alphabet down the side of a sheet of paper, so that you can fill in the *easy* ones first. When you both get stuck, ask some other people for ideas.

Listing words in alphabetical order is a useful dictionary skill. By having to order words that they have chosen, the children are having to use their knowledge of the alphabet, which is an important precursor to understanding how to use a dictionary.

_____and
child

_____
helper(s)

did this activity together

Spelling and phonics

Alphabet vehicles

- Can you think of a vehicle to go with each letter of the alphabet? (You may need to cheat on a few of the letters, for example a **zippy moped** for **z**).

- Write down each letter and draw pictures of the vehicles next to the letters.

impact WRITING HOMEWORK

Fat cat and small ball

- Can you think of some more rhyming pairs like fat cat and small ball?

- Write down three pairs and draw pictures to go with them.

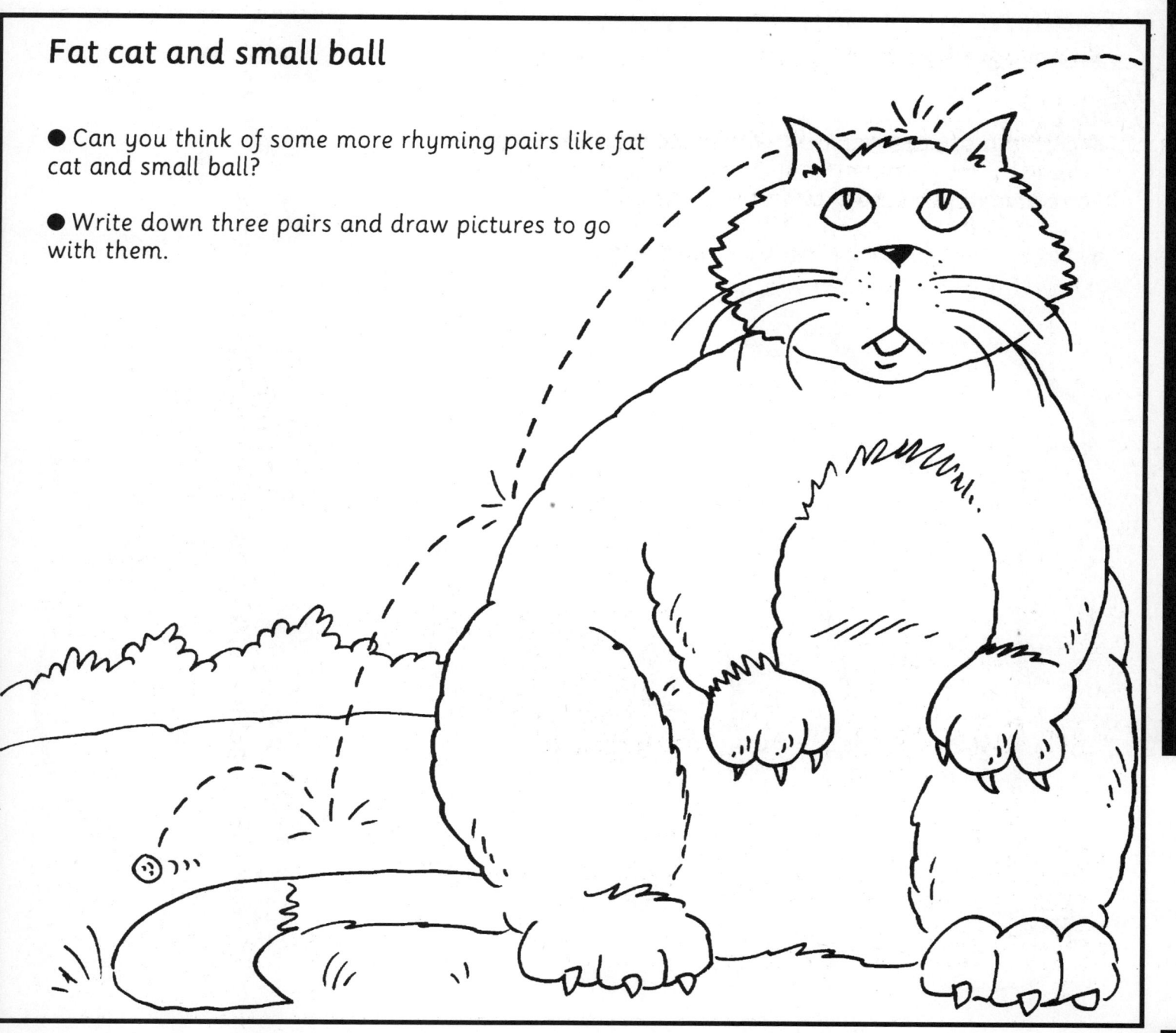

To the helper:
- Talk about the kind of rhymes you might find.
- Talk about the sounds that are the rhyming parts of your rhymes (for example, 'at' and 'all' in the rhyme here). Can you think of any more words with those sounds?

Recognising rhyming words is important in understanding patterns in words, and will help children to guess the spellings of other words when they are writing on their own.

_____and
child

_____
helper(s)

_____

did this activity together

impact WRITING HOMEWORK

Spelling and phonics

To the helper:

- Write the numbers out down the side of a page to start off the activity; and then together think of a rhyming word. Your child could then write down the word next to each number. The fact that the word rhymes is more important than how it is spelled in this activity, although you could talk about how some words look the same but are pronounced differently, and vice versa.

Noticing which words rhyme often gives children a clue as to how to spell the words, so we shall take the activity further in developing children's spelling in class.

_____ and
child

_____
helper(s)

did this activity together

Spelling and phonics

Number rhymes

- Can you count up to five finding words which rhyme?

For example, **'One bun, two shoes...'**

- Write down your rhyme with your helper.

impact WRITING HOMEWORK

Animal names

● Use each letter of your name to start the name of some animals. For example:

M onster
a nt
t ortoise
t arantula
h ippo
e lephant
w arthog

S nake
o strich
p ig
h orse
i guana
e el

To the helper:

● Talk about the letters in your child's name; what sounds do they make? Write out your child's name down the side of the page, so that you can then fill in the sound, and write it down as in the examples here. Help with the spelling.

The first letters in a child's name are generally the first ones they learn, and so become very important letters to them. This activity will also reinforce the relationship between a sound and a symbol.

_____and
child

_____
helper(s)

_____
did this activity together

impact WRITING HOMEWORK

Spelling and phonics

To the helper:

● Have a look at the days of the week, and talk about the **pattern** in the words.

Once the children have learned the recurring part in these words, they will then find it much easier to write the whole words by themselves.

_____and

child

_____

helper(s)

_____

did this activity together

Spelling and phonics

Days of the week

Look how easy it is to write the days of the week!

Sun**day**
Mon**day**
Tues**day**
Wednes**day**
Thurs**day**
Fri**day**
Satur**day**

● Can you see which part of the word is the same each time?

● Now put this list away and write down the days of the week with your helper. Let your helper write the first part of the word each time, and you add on the last part that is always the same.

● Draw a ring around your favourite day and draw a picture of what you like to do on that day.

impact WRITING HOMEWORK

Body parts

- Draw a picture of yourself and label as many parts of your body as you can.

- Learn three of these words, so that you can always spell them correctly!

To the helper:
- Talk about all the names for body parts that they know. Label those parts on the picture.
- Give a hand with spelling if necessary.
- You could fill in any more labels that they might not know the names for.
- Choose three words and let your child practise writing them from memory (tackle the longer names in sections).

Labelling and naming are important skills throughout a child's schooling. Learning to commit specific spellings to memory will help capacity to commit spellings to memory in the future.

_____ and
child

_____
helper(s)

did this activity together

impact WRITING HOMEWORK

Spelling and phonics 69

To the helper:

- Talk about your address; can your child remember your address?
- Write out the address for your child as an example. Give a hand with spelling if necessary.

Knowing their own name and address is essential information for children. Using these familiar words to work out how to write words down is a useful early spelling task.

_____ and
child

_____
helper(s)

did this activity together

Address labels

- Make four labels with your name and address on them.
- Decorate these labels, and use them to label four things that you take to school.

Spelling and phonics

Mixed numbers

● Fill in the missing consonants, and write the numbers.

ei___

o_e

_i_e

_i_e

_i_

___ee

__o

_e_e_

_ou_

impact WRITING HOMEWORK

To the helper:

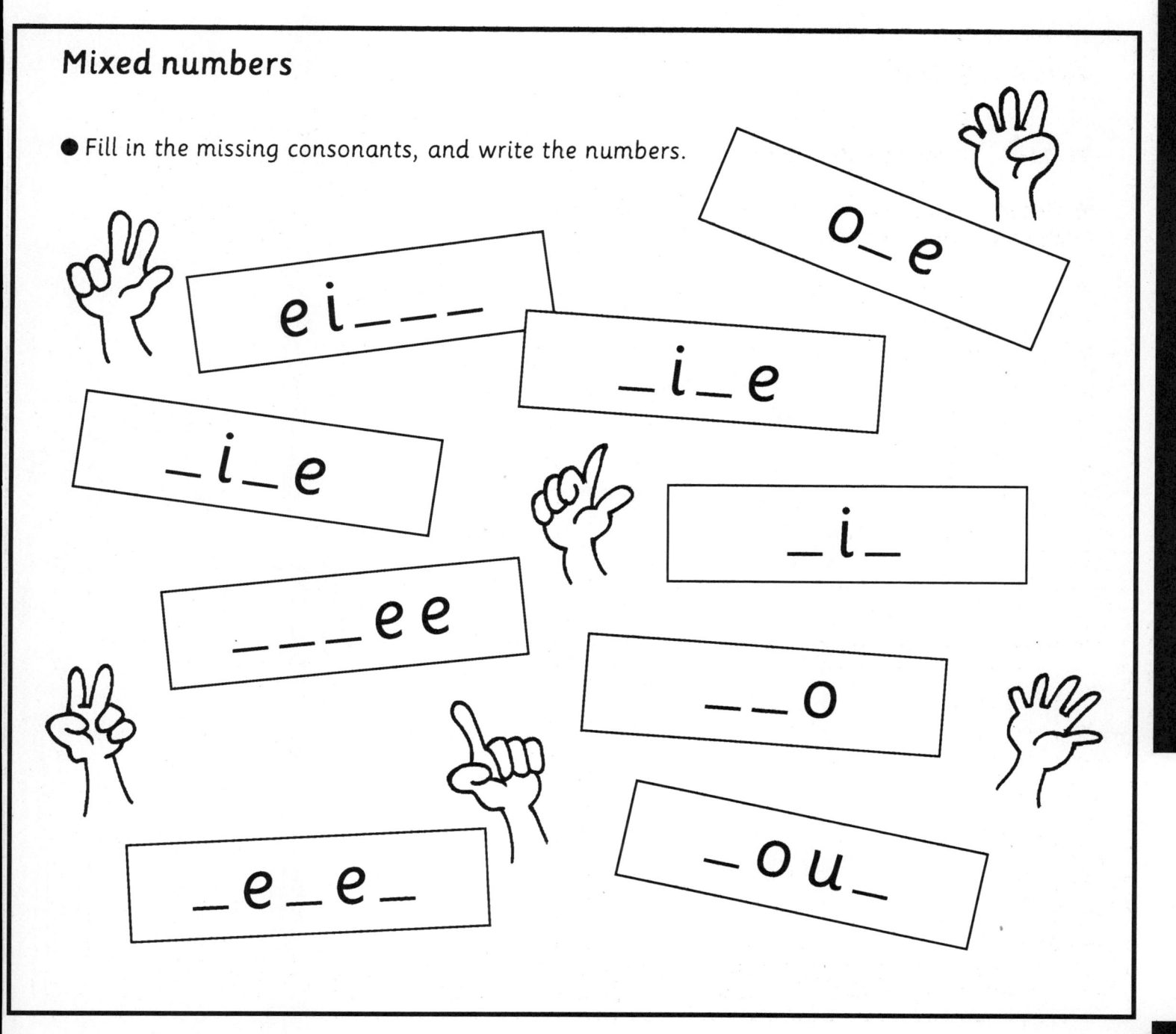

● Talk about the difference between vowels and consonants. Can you guess what the numbers are without filling in the consonants?
● Some words have two consecutive vowels, many have two consecutive consonants. Which words have three consecutive consonants or vowels?

This activity not only helps children focus their attention on the spelling of the numbers, but on the *structure* of words.

_____and
child

_____
helper(s)

_____
did this activity together

Spelling and phonics 71

To the helper:

- Talk about the sounds that animals make when they are expressing these emotions (for example, a cat might go 'ppprrrrrrrrr' when it is happy, and 'schphiiickttt!' when it is angry).
- Talk about how you might write down these sounds: which combinations of letters will make the sound you want the best?

Inventing spellings is an important strategy for children to apply the rules and patterns they have learned about the English language.

_____and
child

_____
helper(s)

_____
did this activity together

Emotional sounds

- Choose an animal and draw it.

- Now draw four different pictures of your animal to make it look happy, sad, angry and scared.

- Write down the word for the sound that comes out of its mouth for each picture.

72 **Spelling and phonics**

impact WRITING HOMEWORK

Greetings

- How many words can you, and anyone else in your house, think of that are used as greetings? For example, **Hi!** or **Hello!**.

- Write down as many as you can.

To the helper:

- There are a great many words and phrases that are used by people to say hello.
- Concentrate on talking about the words, and looking at the spellings once they have been written down.
- Let your child start off with writing, but take over when they have had enough, or get frustrated.

Writing lists is an important skill. It is a quick way of collecting and sorting ideas. This activity also encourages learning to spell useful words. We shall share all our words for hello back in the classroom.

_____and
child

_____
helper(s)

did this activity together

impact WRITING HOMEWORK

Spelling and phonics

To the helper:

- You would be surprised at the number of words and phrases that are used by people to say goodbye – there are quite a few!
- Talk about the words, and look at the spellings together.
- Let your child start off with the writing, but take over when they have had enough, or get frustrated.

Writing lists is an important skill. It is a quick way of collecting and sorting ideas. This activity also encourages learning to spell useful words. We shall share all our words for goodbye back in the classroom.

_____and
child

_____
helper(s)

did this activity together

74   Spelling and phonics

Fare-thee-well

- How many different words can you think of to say goodbye?

- With your helper, make a list.

- Talk about how you write and spell each word.

impact WRITING HOMEWORK

End of the line

- What letters do words **end** with?

- Choose a letter, and find as many words as you can that end with that letter.

To the helper:
- Look through a reading book, or magazine together and point out how some words have the same ending; for example **'-ing', or '-er, or 'es'**.
- When you have decided on a specific ending, go through the book or magazine again to point out relevant words. Your child could write down the words; or you could write down each word, all except for the part which is the same in all of the words — let your child write that part.

By learning the recurring part in these words, they will find it much easier to write the whole words by themselves.

_____and
child

_____
helper(s)

_____
did this activity together

impact WRITING HOMEWORK

Spelling and phonics 75

To the helper:

- Talk about the people that you would give a gift to in your family, and help with writing their name down. Talk about the letters in their names.
- Encourage your child to write the 'To, Love from..' themselves each time without looking back (unless to check).

This activity encourages children to commit to memory a few commonly used words, as well as to learn to spell the names of family members. We shall be using the gift tags at school.

_____and

child

_____

helper(s)

_____

did this activity together

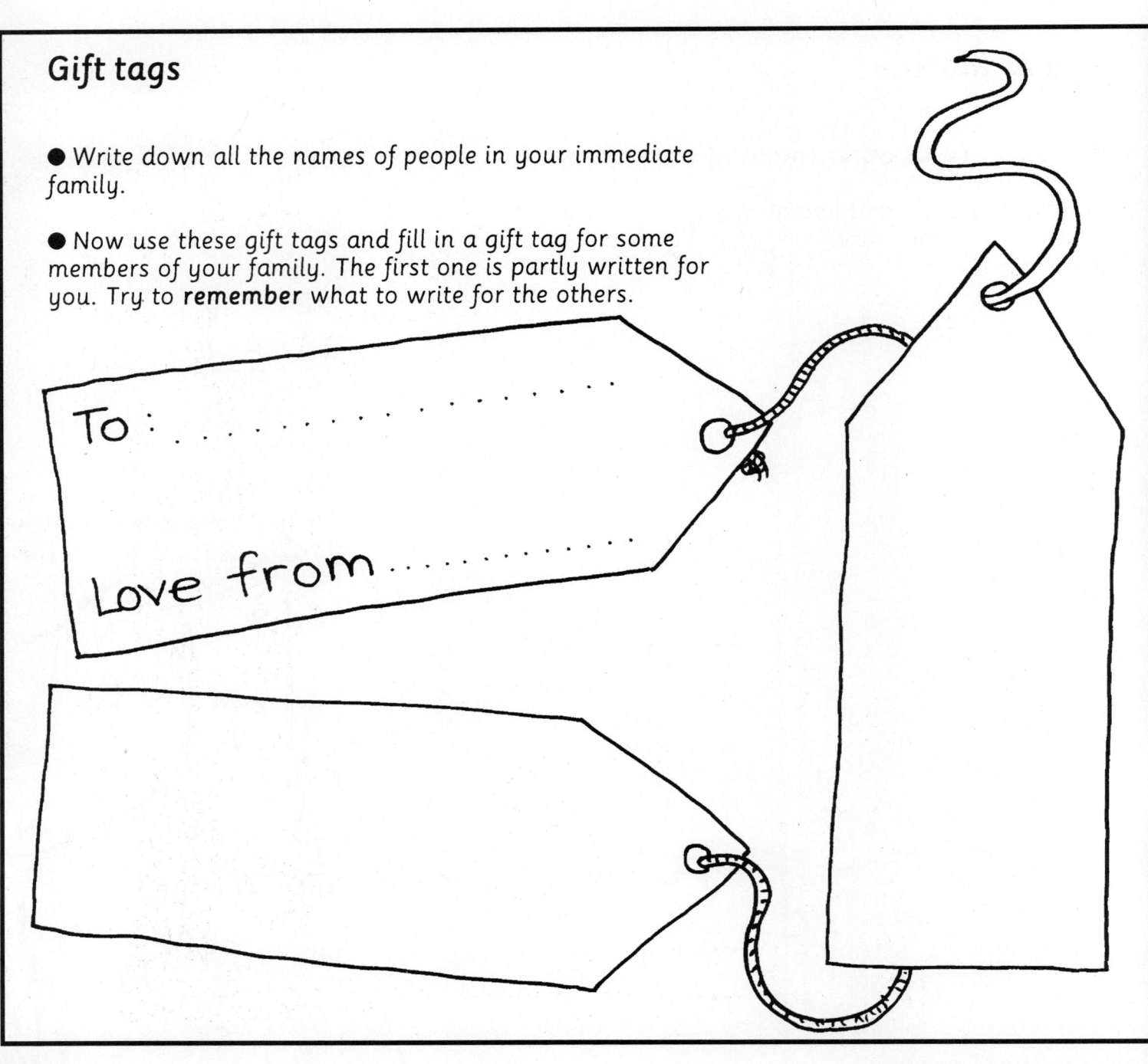

Gift tags

- Write down all the names of people in your immediate family.

- Now use these gift tags and fill in a gift tag for some members of your family. The first one is partly written for you. Try to **remember** what to write for the others.

To: ....

Love from ....

76 Spelling and phonics

impact WRITING HOMEWORK

Abracadabra!

- Invent a new magic word for magicians to use.
- How should it be spelled?
- Write it down.

To the helper:

- Once you have thought of a word you may have to invent a spelling for it. To do this you will have to both listen to the sounds in the word, and then write them down. Tackle the words in sections, so that you can concentrate on the individual sounds, and let your child provide you with the letters to write down.

Inventing spellings is an important strategy for children to apply the rules and patterns they have learned about the English language.

_____ and
child

_____
helper(s)

did this activity together

impact WRITING HOMEWORK

Spelling and phonics 77

To the helper:

- Talk together about other words which begin with the same letter.
- Encourage interesting ways of decorating the letter.

This activity helps children focus on the initial letters and the sounds they make. We shall use the decorated letters which the children bring in to try to make a complete alphabet of illuminated letters. We shall also be practising saying the alphabet in order.

_____ and

child

_____

helper(s)

did this activity together

Illuminated letters

In the Middle Ages the monks who wrote out books by hand used to decorate the first letter of each page. So the **Book of Kells** and the **Winchester Bible** have beautiful illuminated letters to start each page.

● Use your initial letter to make a picture. Draw it and decorate it to make it really beautiful.

Try to use things in your picture which begin with the same letter.

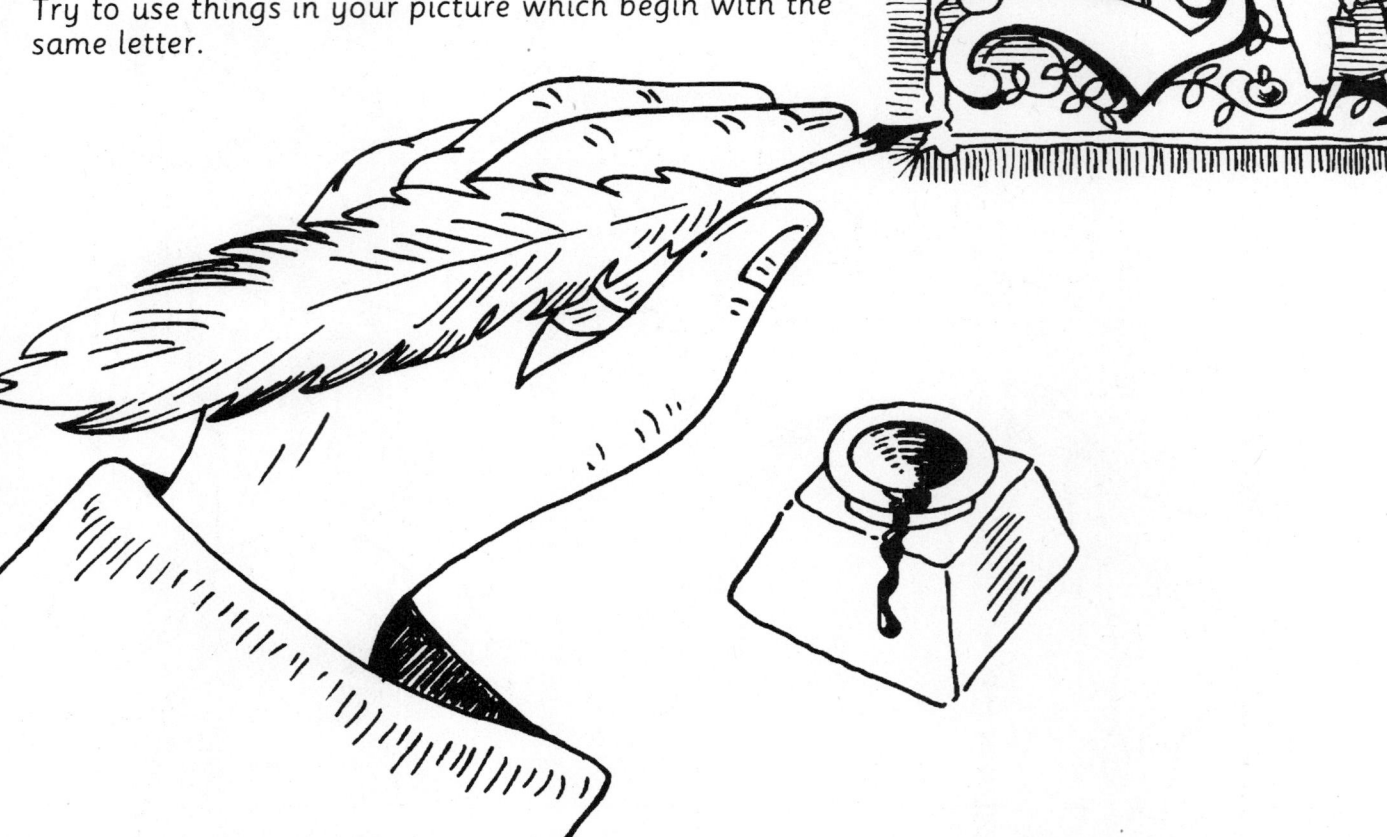

78   **Spelling and phonics**

impact WRITING HOMEWORK

Turn about

- Take it in turn with your helper to think of some words.

- Can you think of a word beginning with 'a'?

Next your helper thinks of a word beginning with 'b'.

Now it's your turn again.

Keep playing until you get to 'z'!

To the helper:

- You will need to help your child remember the alphabet. They will almost certainly forget which letter comes next! This is quite normal. Keep prompting them!!

This activity helps children focus on the initial letter of words and the sounds they make as well as reinforcing the order of the alphabet. We shall make an alphabetical list and learn how to spell some of the words. We shall also practise saying our alphabet!

_____and
child

_____
helper(s)

_____

did this activity together

impact WRITING HOMEWORK

Spelling and phonics

To the helper:

- You will need to help your child remember the alphabet, and to write it down. This is quite normal.
- Help them to think of names by sounding out each letter in turn.

This activity helps children focus on the initial letters of words and the sounds they make. We shall make an alphabetical list of names and talk about all the differences. We shall also practise saying our alphabet!

_____ and

child

_____

helper(s)

_____

did this activity together

Alphabet names

- Write down the alphabet in order.

- Think of a name which begins with each letter of the alphabet. Forexample, **Anne** begins with '**a**', **Ben** begins with '**b**' and so on. Try to find a name for every letter!

80 Spelling and phonics

impact WRITING HOMEWO

Coded alphabet

Here is the alphabet.

a	b	c	d		
e	f	g	h		
i	j	k	l	m	n
o	p	q	r	s	t
u	v	w	x	y	z

- Code each letter according to its row, and how far along the row it is. For example, m is 3.5 because it is in the third row and is 5 along.

- Can you write your name in code. Now write a message. Can your helper translate it? Can your helper write a message to you?

- What do these words say?

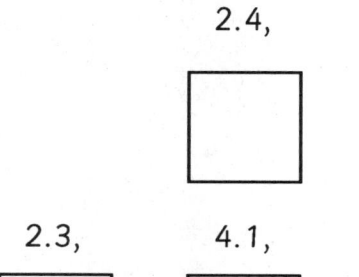

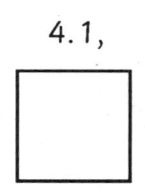

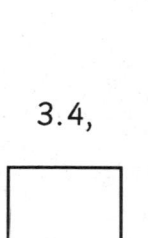

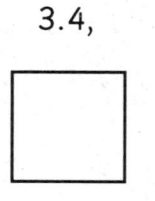

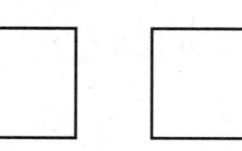

2.4, 2.1, 3.4, 3.4, 4,1

2.3, 4.1, 4.1, 1.4, 1.2, 5.5, 2.1

To the helper:

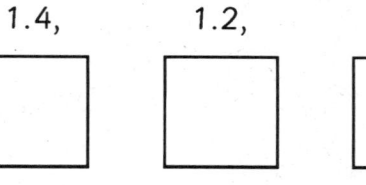

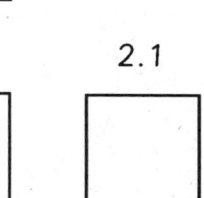

- They will almost certainly need someone to check their codings!

This activity helps children to focus on the alphabet in detail. We shall use some of the discussions to help us develop spelling strategies.

_____ and
child

_____
helper(s)

did this activity together

Spelling and phonics 81

To the helper:

- You will need to help your child remember all the alphabet in order.
- Help them to write a number under each letter – it may help if you write the numbers. The numbers do not necessarily have to be in order from 1–26.

This activity helps children focus on spelling our names and those of our families. We shall also practise saying our alphabet!

_____and

child

_____

helper(s)

_____

did this activity together

Code names

- Write down the alphabet.
- Write a number under each letter. You will need to use the numbers from 1–26!

a												
1												

- Now write your name in code! Write down some of your family's names in code as well. Make sure you spell them correctly!

Secret names

- Write down the alphabet.

- Write your name in code by writing the letter which comes before the letter that should be there. (If you have an **A** in your name write a **Z** from the end of the alphabet.)

For example, **Annie** becomes **zmmhd**!
Sam becomes **Rzl**!

To the helper:

- You will need to help your child remember the alphabet, and to write it down.
- Help them to translate their name into code, and those of other people in their family as well!

This activity helps children to focus on how we write our names. We shall make an alphabetical list of names and talk about all the differences. We shall also practise saying our alphabet!

_____ and
child

_____
helper(s)

did this activity together

Spelling and phonics

To the helper:

- You will need to help your child work out which letter comes first, second, etc. in the backwards name!

This activity helps children to focus on how we spell our names. We shall make an alphabetical list of names and talk about all the differences. We shall also practise saying our alphabet!

_____ and

child

_____

helper(s)

_____

did this activity together

84   Spelling and phonics

Backwards names

- Write down your name.
- Now write your name backwards.
- Can you say this word out loud?
- Draw a picture of yourself upside down to go with it.

For example, **nhoJ** is **John!**
             ymmaS is **Sammy.**

impact WRITING HOMEWO[RK]

Common words

● Talk to your family about which are the five words we use most commonly. Write them down with your helper.

To the helper:

● You will need to talk together about the common words. Which words do you think are common? Which are rare?

This activity will help us to compile a class list of the most commonly used words. The children can then learn how to spell them. This will help them with their own writing!

_____ and
child

_____
helper(s)

_____

did this activity together

Spelling and phonics

To the helper:

● You will need to help your child remember the alphabet, and to find all the letters in the newspaper.

● Try to find an example of each letter in its lower case (ie. not capital) form.

This activity helps children to focus on the letters in and the order of the alphabet. We shall be practising saying our alphabet in school.

_____and

child

_____

helper(s)

_____

did this activity together

Newspaper alphabet

● Using a newspaper, find all the letters of the alphabet. Now cut out one of each letter.

● Paste them on to a piece of paper – in the right order!

86 **Spelling and phonics**

impact WRITING HOMEWORK

Three letter guess

- Think of a three letter word.

- Give your helper a clue.
For example, it is an animal.

- See how many questions your helper has to ask you before the word is known.

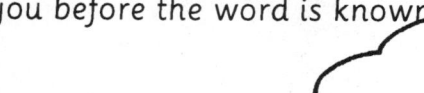

- Now play it the other way round. Your helper thinks of a three-letter word, and gives you a clue. How many questions do you need to ask?

- Play several times.
- Write down some of the words you chose.

To the helper:
- You will need to help your child think up some three-letter words. They may need some help in giving you a clue.
- Try to ask very pointed questions!

This activity helps children to focus on both spelling and vocabulary. We shall be making a note of how you spell the common three-letter words to increase our vocabulary.

_____and
child

_____
helper(s)

_____

did this activity together

impact WRITING HOMEWORK

Spelling and phonics   87

To the helper:

- How many syllables does your child's name have? Help your child beat out their name.
- Decide which station name it matches and write the name near one of the stations.

This activity helps children to focus on the number of syllables in each word. In school we are looking at the structure of different words. This helps us to develop strategies for learning how to spell them.

_____ and
child

_____
helper(s)

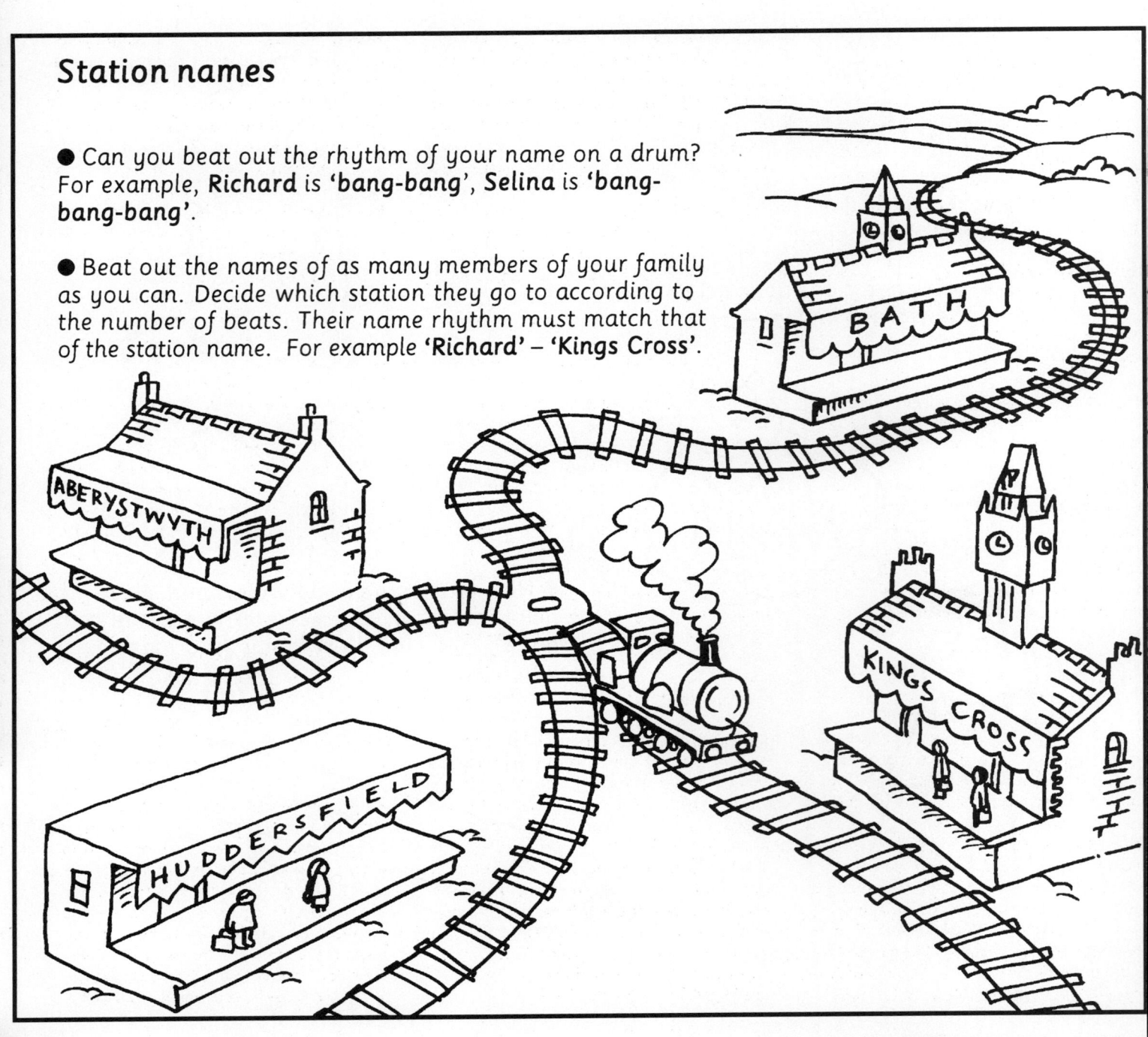

did this activity together

Station names

- Can you beat out the rhythm of your name on a drum? For example, **Richard** is **'bang-bang'**, **Selina** is **'bang-bang-bang'**.

- Beat out the names of as many members of your family as you can. Decide which station they go to according to the number of beats. Their name rhythm must match that of the station name. For example **'Richard'** – **'Kings Cross'**.

88 **Spelling and phonics**

impact WRITING HOMEWORK

Teachers' Notes
YEAR TWO

Breakfast words Collect and display all the children's words. Can you put them in alphabetical order together? The children can then make a dictionary of breakfast words, writing an explanation for each word.

Silly sentences Add any letter of your choice to the worksheet before sending it home. Afterwards look at the children's silly sentences – ask the children to illustrate them. Display the pictures alongside the sentences. Find some tongue twisters to say together, for example 'Peter Piper picked a peck of pickled peppers', 'She sells sea shells on the sea shore', 'Red lorry yellow lorry' etc. What are the sounds that appear most frequently in these sentences?

Silent letters Collect all the silent letters the children have found. How do they vary? When is a 'b' or 'h' or 'w' or 'k' silent? Are there any words in which they are not silent? Did the children find any surprises? (Were there words in which they had not realised that there was a silent letter at all?) Talk about the 'magic e' and how it can change the sound of a whole word eg. 'at' - 'ate', 'car' - 'care' etc.

Onomatopoeia Collect up all the onomatopoeias the children have collected. Paint pictures to go with the words – eg. a splash of water with 'Splash!' written on it; a cat with a speech bubble 'Miaow!', a balloon exploding 'Bang!'. Get the children to draw the pictures and write the words – big and clearly so everyone can read

them. Read through them all together. Try writing short poems using the words the children have thought of.

Collecting 'ing'/Do-ing at home Read through some of the examples the children have brought in. Write them up on a board or sheet of paper that all the children can see. Use two coloured pens. You write up the first part of the word in, say, red; and the children can fill in the ending '-ing' in blue. Talk about words that need to be changed before you add the '-ing'. For example, 'write' loses its 'e' before you add '-ing'; 'run' becomes 'running' with a double 'n' etc.

Two, to or too? Write down the three spellings of 'to'. Read them together and ask the children if they can remember the different meanings. Write the children's examples on the board. Whenever you come across one of the 'to's' in any reading with the children, point out the word and the context.

A hoard of boards Write down the children's words on a display. Ask the children to underline the rhyming part in the words with a coloured pen. Use another coloured pen to underline the words that are all spelled '-oard'. How can you make the sound using different spellings? For example, 'cord', 'Maud', 'applaud' or 'bored'.

Fright night Write down the children's words on a display. Ask the children to underline the rhyming part in the words with a coloured pen. Use another coloured pen to underline the words that are all spelled '-ight'. How can you make the sound using different spellings? For example, 'site', 'mite' or 'kite', etc.

Eeek! Write down the children's words on a display. Ask the children to underline the rhyming part in the words with a coloured pen. Use another coloured pen to underline the words that are all spelled '-eek'. How can you make the sound using different spellings? For example, 'leak'.

Word chains You can continue playing this game in the classroom. You could use the children's names: Paul, Lisa, Amrit, Tom etc. Write the words on the board, and talk about the word chain – beginnings and endings of words. Perhaps you will find words that end in blends, eg. 'ch', 'st', 'th' etc. which will also start words.

Food word chain This will be useful to start off a topic on food or eating. Continue playing this game in the classroom; you could use any words not just foods. Play together, writing the words on the board, and talk about the word chain – beginnings and endings of words. Perhaps you will find words that end in blends, eg. 'ch', 'st', 'th' etc. which will also start words.

Animal word chain This will be useful to start off a topic on animals. Continue playing this game in the classroom; you could use any words not just animals. Play together, writing the words on the board, and talk about the word chain – beginnings and endings of words. Perhaps you will find words that end in blends, eg. 'ch', 'st', 'th' etc. which will also start words.

Verb word chain Continue playing this game in the classroom. It might be easier just to think of any words rather than focusing on just verbs. Write the words on the board, and talk about the word chain – beginnings and endings of words. Perhaps you will find words that end in blends, eg. 'ch', 'st', 'th' etc. which will also start words. Talk about 'doing' words (see the notes on 'Collect -ing' for some ideas).

Adjective word chain Continue playing this game in the classroom. It might be easier just to think of any words rather than focusing on just adjectives. Write the words on the board, and talk about the word chain – beginnings and endings of words. Perhaps you will find words that end in blends, eg. 'ch', 'st', 'th' etc. which will also start words. Talk about describing words, and see how many you can all

come up with – this may be a useful resource for any future creative writing.

Forget-me-not Look at the word families amongst the collection of words; for example 'th' words, thingummy, thing, thingamajig... etc. How do we spell them? What do they all have in common? Make a list of the common words. Look at cultural differences – do different cultures have different ways of expressing this? Do any of the words we use come from other languages originally?

Four-letter word chain Play this game in class with the children. Talk about the difficulties they might have had sticking to the limit of four letters. Choose a blend that appears in your game for example 'th' words, and try to find as many words as you can that begin with that sound. Can you find any words with '-th' at the end (eg. path, pith)?

Colour rhymes How many colours did the children find to rhyme with? Did anyone use alternative names for colours; for example vermilion for red, ochre for yellow, jade for green. Describe colours with rhyming words – mellow yellow, pink sink, black crack. Value the 'near-rhymes' that the children come up with, for example 'burple purple'. Get the children to use coloured felt-tipped pens to write silly sentences all rhyming with the colour they are using. For example 'The yellow fellow played his mellow cello'.

Hobby words Ask the children to bring in something to do with their hobby and to remember one word connected with the hobby with its spelling. They can then make a mini presentation to the rest of the class. Get them to write the word they have learned on the board. Can they remember any of the other words?

Blended sounds Leave a sheet of paper displayed where the children can reach, with 'bl' written in the middle, and a few examples to start them off. The children can

Spelling and phonics

then fill in their own 'bl' words. Sort the other blends the children have thought of – you could replace the sheet every few days with these other blends.

Syllable count up Make sure the children understand what a syllable is before you send this activity home. You can play clapping games with the children to reinforce the syllables in the words. We make supercallifragilisticexpealidocious 14 syllables. Try thinking of long words together before they try this at home. When the words come back into class, write them up on a sheet of paper or the board and read them through – count the syllables together. Who has thought of the longest word? Does it have the most syllables?

Mixed-teens Before this activity goes home make sure the children have some idea of the difference between vowels and consonants. Write down a few numbers and talk about the letters. Look at words with two consecutive consonants – blends, any words with three consecutive vowels or consonants. Use the fact that the children will be more familiar with reading the names of the teen numbers to help with any maths number work.

Word stairs Continue playing this game in the classroom. Play together on the carpet; writing the words on the board, and talk about the word chain – beginnings and endings of words.

Moon Try this activity out at school first – what word pairs do the children think of? Start off with a few examples; house and mouse, ring and sing. Look at the endings. Do they find any rhyming words that are spelled differently? For example, cheap and sleep. Once the children bring in their word pairs you can talk about how the words are spelled – write a few of the word pairs (with matching endings) on the board.

Suffix Make a list of all the things the children in the class are – e.g. climbers, runners, players, actors etc. Talk about the issue of gender; sometimes we have female forms of words, such as actor/actress, manager/manageress. To encourage the children's spelling techniques, look at how many of their words can be made into 'ing' words. E.g. climbing, running, playing etc. Talk about 'doing' words or verbs.

Phone shop Make a list of all the words. Now try a group activity to do with different sounds, e.g. 'st' or 'ch' or 'th' or 'sp'. Each group has a pile of books. How many words can they find starting with their sound? Make lists and talk about the words which rhyme, and the words which are the same apart from their starting sound like 'chair' and 'stair'.

Tele-tele! Make a class list of all the words. Talk about the meanings of all the different words. Make a 'tele' display, by letting the children draw pictures and write definitions of some of their words. Look at the structure of the words. Can the children find other words which end with the same part, if you take off the 'tele' prefix, e.g. tele-phone/head-phone.

Double o Make a class list of all the words that the children have managed to find. Talk about the meaning of all the different words. Were there any which no-one had heard of before? Let each child choose one of the words on the list and write a definition for it, and draw a picture to go with it. Make a display. Put the children into groups and ask some of them to find 'ee' words and some to find 'ui' words and some to find 'ea' words and some to find 'a' words. Give each group a pile of books to help them. How long a list can they each make?

Rhyming animals Play a game using the children's rhyming pairs. Use the hall, or push back the chairs in your classroom. Prepare stickers, each with one animal of a rhyming pair on them. Muddle the stickers up and stick one on each child. They have to read their sticker, and find their partner.

Rhyming sentence Get the children to read out their silly sentences. Illustrate them altogether with cartoon pictures and display them with the sentences. Does anyone in the class have a matching sound in their name? Look closely at one of the children's sentences on the board, and get another one of the children to underline the words that rhyme. Are they spelled the same? Are there any patterns in the spelling?

Star light, star bright Put all the rhymes in a book that the children can go to and read in their own time. Get the children to write their own rhymes out in their own books, and to underline the rhyming sound that recurs throughout the rhyme. Write out the sound. Does anyone else have a matching rhyming sound? Write down as many words as you can that rhyme with your sound.

Spellcheck Talk with the children before this activity goes home about the kind of words you would like them to remember. Are there any words that are *always* being spelled wrongly in your class? Look at the bookmarks the children make at home – it might be a good idea to have these to hand when the children are writing. They can then add any other words they have difficulty with to the list as they go. Talk about the *strategies* you might use to help you choose the correct spelling of a word. For example, you might write down a few different spellings and choose the one that 'looks right'. Or you might look up the word in a dictionary (if you are sure of the first few letters).

Valentine message Use the messages to make Valentine cards. Emphasise to the children that the message can be for *anyone*, not just a boy or girlfriend. It could be for a sister, Dad, Mum, brother, Gran, to you even. Try thinking of a few examples in class together.

Dragon's teeth
Photocopy and enlarge a copy of the dragon's head from the activity sheet. You can use this to play the game as a whole class, so the children have a good idea of what to do before the activity goes home! Once the children have played the game a few times at home you can then use the game in the class; photocopy a few sheets with the dragon's head on them to that the children can play the game at school. Talk about the difference between vowels and consonants – are there any letters which frequently occur in words? Talk about the strategies the children use to solve the mystery words.

Newspaper words Can the children remember where their words come from? Have they used words from titles of articles, from adverts etc.? Put the children in pairs or threes and get them to cut out their words again, and try to sort all 20/30 words into alphabetical order. Talk to the children about sorting words which have the same initial letter as one another – look at the second and maybe the third letters to put them in alphabetical order.

Spot the missing letters Try a few 'missing letters' with the children before the activity goes home; and talk about the sound that the missing letters make. How did the children guess the missing letters? When the children bring back their sentences; get them to swap with a friend and try to find the letters. What sounds do the missing letters make? Think of three more words that have those missing letters in them (from just one word; then the children can choose).

More than one Collect together all the 'odd' plurals that the children have found. Ask the children to help you arrange them in alphabetical order and make a class list.

Breakfast words

- Collect five words that you can see on a **cereal packet**.

You could either cut them out from the packet, or copy them down.

- Can you put them in alphabetical order?

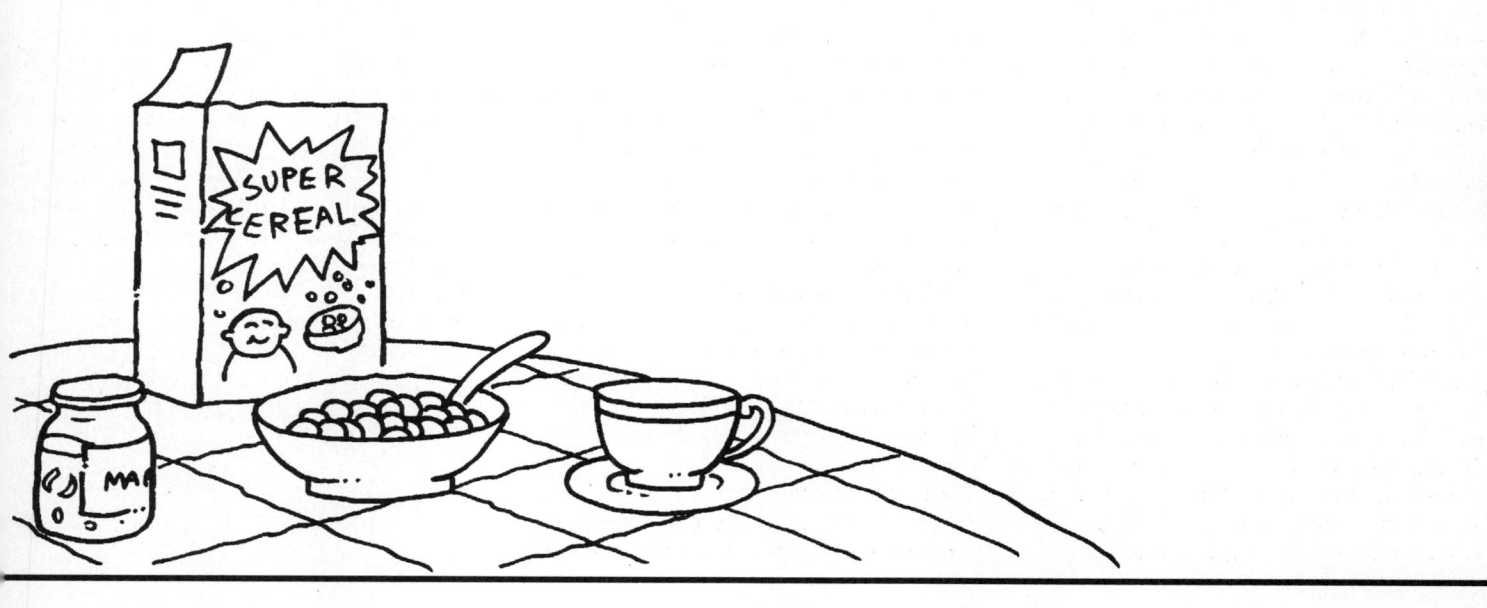

To the helper:

- Make sure your child has five words. Help with reading them if needed.
- Write out an alphabet strip (a to z in a line), so your child can refer to it.
- Sort the words on a first letter only basis, and then look at words that need further sorting (two words such as **Kelloggs** and **Krispies** need to be ordered by their first *and* second letter).

This activity practises a useful skill, in which the children exercise their knowledge of the alphabet; a precursor to using dictionaries. Back in class we shall try to find these words in the dictionary.

_____ and
child

_____
helper(s)

did this activity together

Spelling and phonics

To the helper:

- First think about the sound, and all the things you can think of beginning with that sound. This will give you a selection of words to play with.
- If the sentence gets very long you may have to help with the writing.

Writing alliterative nonsense sentences allows the children to 'play' with the sounds of words in the English language without having to worry about making sense; in fact the more nonsensical they are, the more fun it will be to read them!

_____ and

child

_____

helper(s)

did this activity together

Silly sentences

'The slippery sausage slid smoothly into the slithery spaghetti.'

This is a silly sentence using **'s'** as the first sound of most of the words.

- Write another silly sentence using _____ as your sound.

Spelling and phonics

impact WRITING HOMEWO

Silent letters

- Look in your reading book for as many words as you can that have silent letters. Final **e** does not count.

- Write the words down.

- Can your helper add any to your list?

To the helper:

- Talk about what a silent letter is; for example **k** in '**k**not' or '**k**nitting'; the **w** in '**w**ho' etc.
- Look through your child's reading book carefully and read out the words together. Look at the words closely and see if you can spot any letters that do not make a sound in the word.

The children are looking at the words in a text very closely, and recognise the sounds made by the letters in the words. We shall share all the 'silent letter' words back in class, and see if we can find any patterns.

_____and

child

_____

helper(s)

did this activity together

impact WRITING HOMEWORK

Spelling and phonics

To the helper:

- You may need to start this activity off with a few ideas of your own; these can be quite difficult to find.

Onomatopoeias are special words in the English language, and this activity gives the children a chance to focus on them exclusively. We shall share the children's examples of onomatopoeias back at school, and this collection of words can then be used to help us write poetry.

_____ and
child

_____
helper(s)

did this activity together

94   Spelling and phonics

Onomatopoeia

- An onomatopoeic word is a word that sounds like the thing it is describing. For example, **splash**, or **miaow**. See if you can find any of these in your reading book, or can you think of any yourself?

- Write down your words with a picture to illustrate each sound.

- Can you helper think of any more?

impact WRITING HOMEWORK

Collecting 'ing'

- Using your reading book, find as many words as you can that end in 'ing'. Write them down.

- Can you think of any more 'ing' words?

To the helper:
- Start off the activity by giving your child a few examples of **'ing'** words.
- Look through the book together, and help your child spot words, but if they get tired you might want to share the writing. If you find a word (or think of one) you could write down the first part of the word, and let your child complete the **'ing'** part.

By isolating a common word ending, and concentrating on it, the children are far more likely to spot it when they are reading, and more likely to spell it correctly when they are writing independently.

_____and
child

_____
helper(s)

did this activity together

Spelling and phonics

To the helper:

- Talk about doing words (verbs); give a few examples to start off the discussion.
- Share the writing so that you write down the first part of the first word, for example, **play**, and then your child can fill in the **ing**. For the next word your child writes the first half, and you write the **ing**. And so on.

By isolating a common word ending, and concentrating on it, the children are far more likely to spot it when they are reading, and even more likely to spell it correctly when they are writing independently.

Do-ing it at home

- Think of some things people do at home.

For example: cooking, cleaning.

- Write down ten examples of do-ing words in the form of a list.

- Take turns with your helper to write the first or second half of each word (the second half always being the **-ing**).

_____ and
child

_____
helper(s)

_____
did this activity together

96 **Spelling and phonics**

Two, to or too?

- Find three sentences from your reading book, or make sure that you use the right words each time!

- Ask your helper to think of some, too.

To the helper:

- Suggest a sentence for each example, and write it down so that your child can see the differences.
- Look through the reading book for ideas, or think of some of your own.
- Try and think of a sentence that combines all three types of **to**.

This focuses the children on a specific part of the English language. Although the words sound the same, they have very different meanings, and children can be confused by which spelling is for which meaning. Later the children should remember when to use each of the different spellings.

_____and

child

_____

helper(s)

_____

did this activity together

impact WRITING HOMEWORK

Spelling and phonics 97

To the helper:

- Start off the activity by giving your child a few examples of rhyming words – you could even write them down so that they can see what they are looking for.
- Look through the book together, and help your child spot the words.
- Let your child write down the words, but if they get tired you could share the writing.

By isolating a common sound, and focusing on it, the children are far more likely to spot any patterns when they are reading, and even more likely to spell them correctly when writing independently.

_____and
child

_____
helper(s)

did this activity together

A hoard of boards

- Hunt in your reading book for as many words as you can that rhyme with **board**. They can be spelled differently but they must rhyme.

- Ask your helper to think of some more.

98 Spelling and phonics

impact WRITING HOMEWORK

Fright night!

- Hunt in your reading book for as many words as you can that rhyme with **night**. They can be spelled differently but they must rhyme.

- Ask your helper to think of some more.

To the helper:
- Before you look in the reading book, start off the activity by giving your child a few examples of rhyming words – you could even write them down so that they can see what they are looking for.
- Let your child write down the words but if they get tired share the writing.

Isolating a common sound, and concentrating on it, enables children to recognise word patterns when they are reading. It also helps to spell words correctly in independent writing.

_____ and
child

_____
helper(s)

_____
did this activity together

Spelling and phonics

To the helper:

- Before looking in the reading book, start the activity by giving your child some examples of rhyming words – maybe write them down so that they can see what they are looking for.
- Look through the book together, and help your child spot words.
- Let your child write down the words but if they get tired you could share the writing.

By isolating a common sound, and focusing on it, the children are far more likely to spot any patterns when they are reading, and even more likely to spell them correctly when they are writing independently.

_____and

child

_____

helper(s)

_____

did this activity together

Spelling and phonics

Eeek!

- Hunt in your reading book for as many words as you can that rhyme with **seek**. They can be spelled differently but they must rhyme.

- Ask your helper to think of some more.

impact WRITING HOMEWORK

Word chains

- Choose any word from your reading book and write it down.

- Ask your helper to write down a word that begins with the last letter of your word.

- Now it's your turn again to find a word that begins with the last letter of your helper's word.

- Make a word chain: **rabbit – tree – end – dog...** keep going!

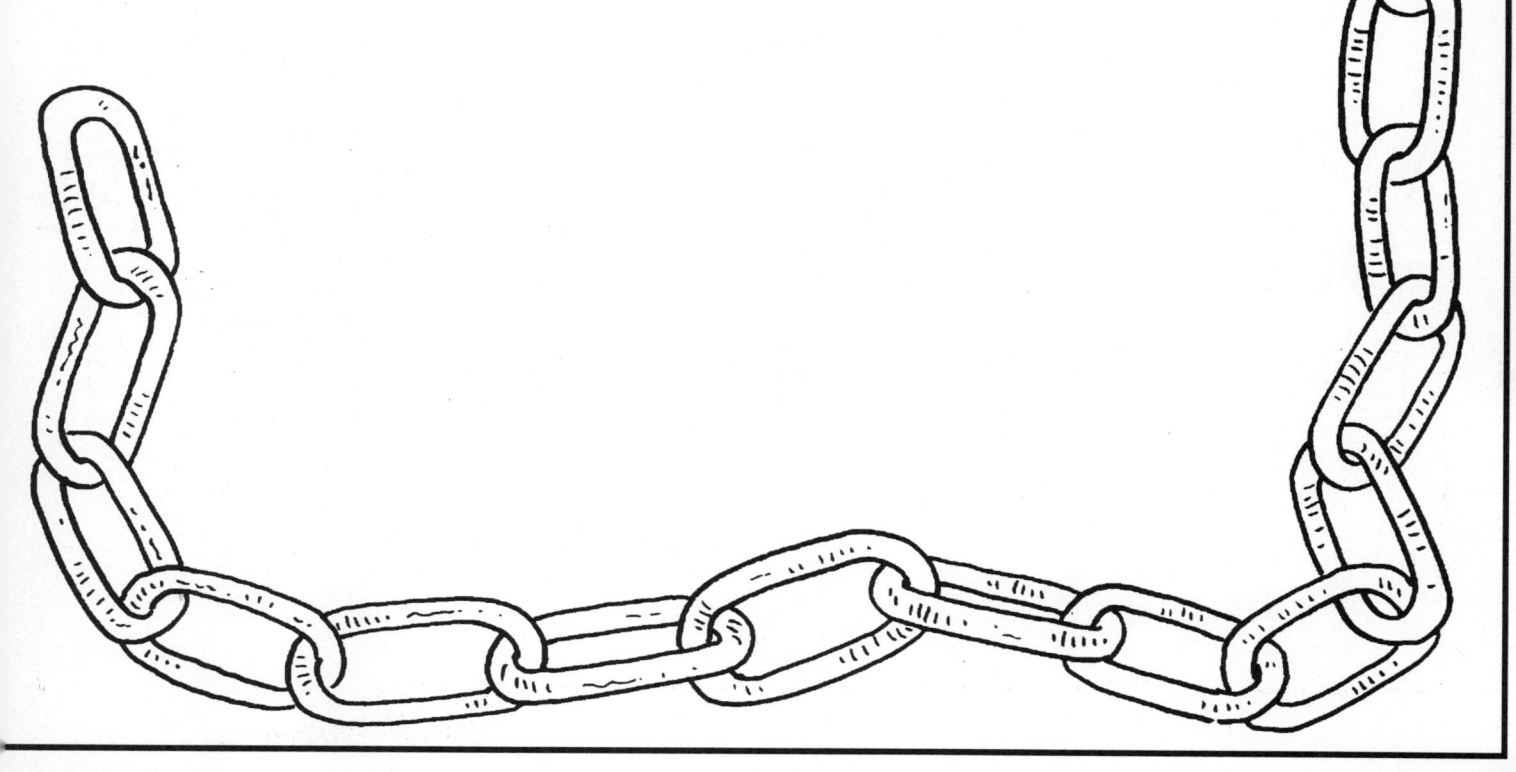

To the helper:

- Write down the words, taking it in turns, as it will be much easier to see on paper which is the last letter, and so the first letter of the next word.

This activity focuses on beginnings and endings of words.

_____and
child

_____
helper(s)

did this activity together

Spelling and phonics

To the helper:

- Before you start you could make a list of foods, to help you when you are playing the game. This will also give your child a better idea of the type of words you are looking for.
- Write down the words as it will be much easier to see on paper which is the last letter, and so the first letter of the next word.

This activity has two purposes; thinking about food words, and on beginnings and endings of words.

Food word chain

● Make a chain of **food** words that always start with the last letter of the word before.

For example: **crisp – potato – orange – egg...**

● Write down your chain.

Continue for five minutes, taking it in turns to think of a word. (You might need your helper to be the writer for this.)

_____and
child

_____
helper(s)

_____
did this activity together

102 Spelling and phonics

impact WRITING HOMEWORK

Animal word chain

● Make a chain of **animal** words that always start with the last letter of the word before.

For example: **zebra** – anteater – rat – tiger...

● Write down your chain.

Continue for five minutes, taking it in turns to think of a word. (You might need your helper to be the writer for this.)

To the helper:

● Before you start you could make a list of animals, to help you when you are playing the game. This will also give your child a better idea of the type of words you are looking for.
● Write down the words as it will be much easier to see on paper which is the last letter, and so the first letter of the next word.

This activity has two purposes; thinking about animal words, and on beginnings and endings of words.

_____and
child

_____
helper(s)

did this activity together

Spelling and phonics 103

To the helper:

- Before you start you could make a list of verbs, to help you when you are playing the game. This will give your child a better idea of the type of words you are looking for.
- Write down the words, as it will be much easier to see on paper which is the last letter, and so the first letter of the next word.

This activity has two purposes; focusing on verbs, and on beginnings and endings of words.

Verb word chain

A verb is a **doing** word, an action word.

- Make a chain of verbs that always start with the last letter of the word before.

For example: **watch – hear – read – drive...**

- Write down your verb chain.

Continue for five minutes, taking it in turns with your helper to think of a word. (You might need your helper to be the writer for this.)

_____ and
child

_____
helper(s)

_____
did this activity together

104   Spelling and phonics

impact WRITING HOMEWORK

Adjective word chain

An adjective is a **describing** word. Make a chain of adjectives that always start with the last letter of the word before.

For example: **fast – tall – long – gross...**

● Write down your chain.

● Continue for five minutes, taking it in turns with your helper to think of a word. (You might need your helper to be the writer for this.)

To the helper:

● Before you start you could make a list of adjectives to help you when you are playing the game. This will give your child a better idea of the type of words you are looking for.

● Write down the words as it will be much easier to see on paper which is the last letter, and so the first letter of the next word.

This activity has two purposes; focusing on adjectives, and on beginnings and endings of words.

_____and
child

_____
helper(s)

did this activity together

Spelling and phonics 105

To the helper:

- This could be done as a kind of newspaper report, with your child interviewing people in the house.
- Some of these words may not have a standard spelling, and so you will have to create a spelling for them. To do this listen to the sounds in the word, and then write them down, tackling the words in sections. Let your child think of the letters to write down.

Inventing spellings is an important strategy for children to apply the rules and patterns they have learned about the English language.

_____and
child

_____
helper(s)

_____
did this activity together

Forget-me-not

- Do you ever forget the correct word for something?

- Write what you say to make up for the missing word. For example **Thingummy**.

- Ask other people at home what they say if they can't think of the right word, and write it down.

106   Spelling and phonics

impact WRITING HOMEWORK

Four-letter word chain

Play this game with your helper.

● You are going to make a special word chain. Start by writing down a simple four-letter word, for example **spot**.
Next make a word with the same first two letters (for example, **sp**in).
Now make a word that has the same last two letters (for example, th**in**).
Next make one with the same first two letters (for example, **th**at) and so on.

● Play this game with your helper. It might be fun to get more people involved if you can! Otherwise, swap over after a while so that you are not always stuck with finding the first, or last two letters!

To the helper:

● You may need to demonstrate the game to your child before you start, and to point out what you are doing each time. When they have got the hang of it, then let them make suggestions.

By playing this game, the children are having to notice patterns in spellings, and apply them to words which they already know.

_____and
child

_____
helper(s)

_____

did this activity together

Spelling and phonics 107

To the helper:

- Start by writing down all the colours you can think of before you go through the reading book.

By concentrating on certain word endings, the children are more likely to spot them again when they are reading, and even more likely to spell words correctly when they are writing independently.

_____and

child

_____

helper(s)

did this activity together

Colour rhymes

● How many words can you find in your reading book that rhyme with colour words?

For example: Jack – black
kite – white
who – blue

● Write them down. Draw some pictures to go with your list.

Spelling and phonics

Hobby words

- Draw a picture of yourself doing your favourite hobby or activity.
- Write down five words about your hobby.
- Learn how to spell them all.

To the helper:

- Talk about the activity your child enjoys the most (besides watching TV).
- Write down a selection of words to do with that activity for example, for swimming you might choose: water, costume, goggles... etc).
- Make sure the words are spelled correctly before your child tries to learn them!

Being able to commit specific spellings to memory will obviously help children when they need to write these words down, but the process will also help commit spellings to memory in the future.

_____ and
child

_____
helper(s)

did this activity together

impact WRITING HOMEWORK

Spelling and phonics

To the helper:

- Talk about what a blend is, and try to think of as many **bl** words as you can (you don't need to write these down, unless you want to).
- Now choose your own blend, talk about it and then write down all the ideas you both come up with.

Understanding how blends work through focusing on one particular example is a useful skill for independent writing and having to build words that your child does not necessarily know how to spell.

_____ and
child

_____
helper(s)

did this activity together

Spelling and phonics

Blended sounds

Some words start with blended sounds, for example, bl- in **blends**!

● How many words can you think of that start with **bl**?

● Think of another blended sound and ask your helper to write down a list of words that you have both thought of that begin with that sound.

impact WRITING HOMEWORK

Syllable count up

Supercallifragilisticexpeallidocious!

- How many syllables are there in this word?

- Find the longest word you can and write it down. How many syllables has it got?

To the helper:
- Talk about what a syllable is. How many syllables are there in your child's name? Carefully count how many syllables there are in the word above (clap for each syllable).
- Look in books, newspapers, magazines and dictionaries for long words and count how many syllables there are.

Syllables are an important part of word construction; and this activity raises children's awareness of them. We shall share our long words back in the classroom, and count which word has the most syllables.

_____and
child

_____
helper(s)

_____
did this activity together

Spelling and phonics

To the helper:

- Talk about the difference between vowels and consonants. Can you guess what the numbers are without filling in the consonants?
- Some words have two consecutive vowels, many have two consecutive consonants. Which words have three consecutive consonants or vowels?

This activity not only helps children focus their attention on the spelling of the numbers, but on the *structure* of words.

_____and

child

_____

helper(s)

_____

did this activity together

Mixed-teens

● Fill in the missing consonants, and write the numbers.

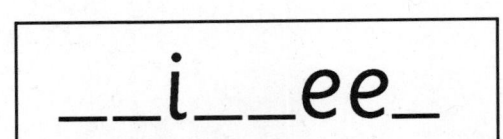

__i__ee_

_ou__ee_

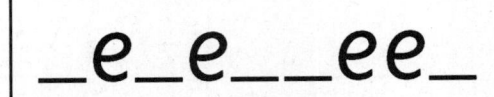

_i__ee_

_i__ee_

_e_e__ee_

ei___ee_

_i_e_ee_

112 Spelling and phonics

impact WRITING HOMEWO

Word stairs

This is a word stair.

s o c k s
       i
       l
       l
       y e l l o w
                 i
                 n
                 d
                 o
                 w

Each word begins with the last letter of the word before.

- How many steps can you make?

To the helper:

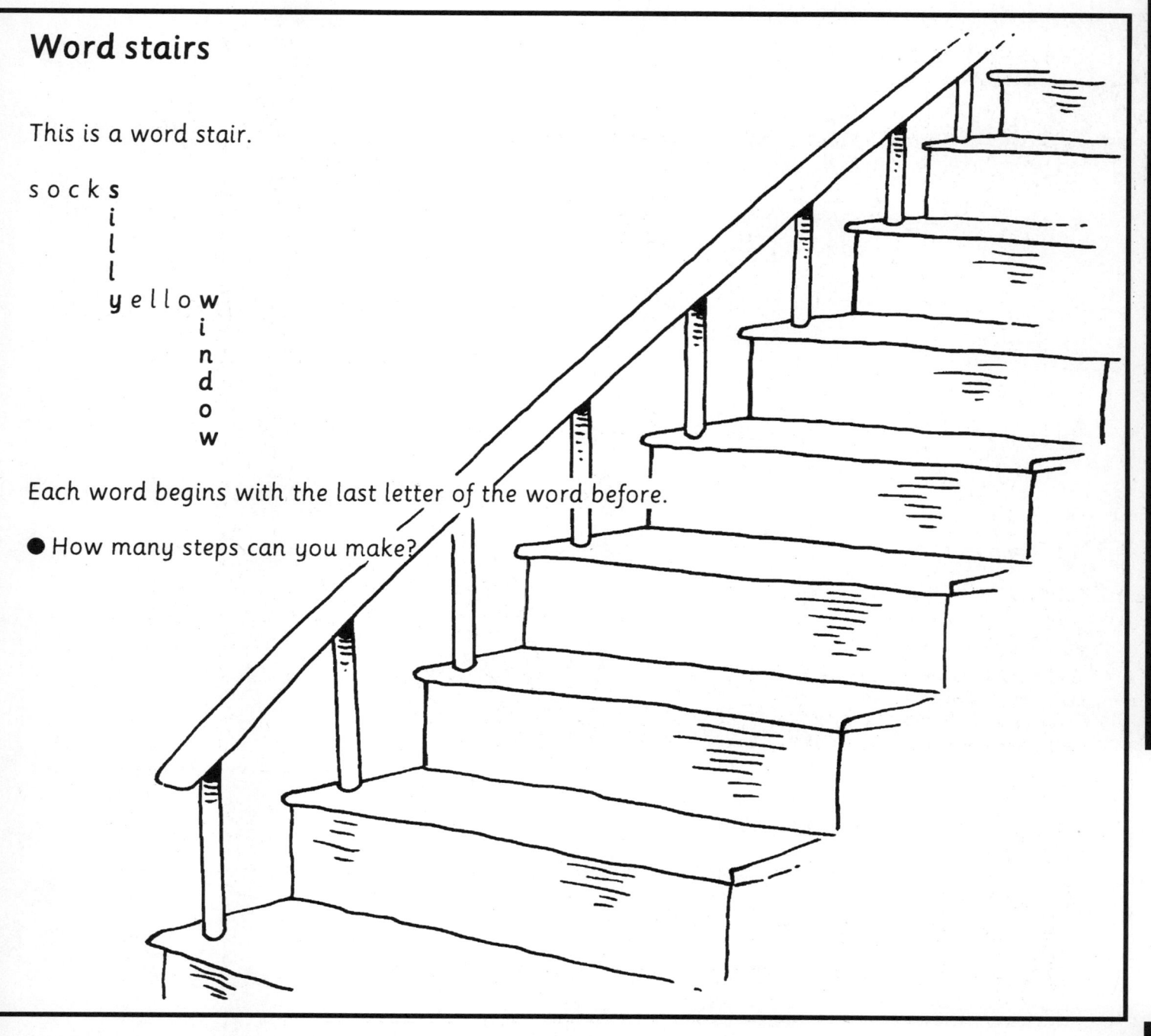

- You could take it in turns to think of words to fit in the word stairs.

Here the children are having to think about the first and last letters of any word, and the number of letters in the word. By having to focus closely on single words at a time, they are also having to remember their spellings.

_____and

child

_____

helper(s)

_____

did this activity together

WRITING HOMEWORK

Spelling and phonics 113

To the helper:

- Choose short three or four letter words, for which the children can write a rhyming word.
- The idea is to discover that some rhyming words are spelled the same, and so predicting the spelling of a rhyming word is quite easy. There are obviously many exceptions, which you could talk about as you come across them.

In learning to spell, children have to learn many conventions, and this activity reveals one of them. If you don't know the spelling for one word, but you do know the spelling for a rhyming word, you can work out the spelling you need.

_____ and

child

_____

helper(s)

_____

did this activity together

Moon

- Write down a word, for example **moon**. Then write down a matching word such as **soon**. Can you spell it?

- Get your helper to write down another word, and then you write down a matching word.

- Try doing this with at least five words.

- Can you see an easy way to do it?

Spelling and phonics

impact WRITING HOMEWORK

Suffix

A suffix is a letter or group of letters added to the end of a word to change the way you use it.

For example: read - **er**

● Make a list with your helper of all the things you can do (for example, **run, climb, think**...).

● Now make another list alongside this list to say what you are because you can do these things.

For example:

climb - climber
run - runner

To the helper:

● Talk about what a suffix is, and see if you can think of any examples.
● Get your child to suggest all the things they think they can do (you can fill in a few), and then they can write out the word again alongside the ones you have written, only this time they add 'er'.

In the process of learning to spell, children have to learn many conventions, and this activity reveals one of them.

_____ and
child

_____
helper(s)

did this activity together

WRITING HOMEWORK — **Spelling and phonics** 115

To the helper:

- Try to think of as many **'ph'** words as you can (you don't need to write these down).
- Now look for **'sh'** words, talk about them and then write down all the ideas.

These are called consonant digraphs. When the two consonants are used together they make a completely different sound. Should words such as 'telephone' be written as they are in other countries – 'telefone'?

_____and

child

_____

helper(s)

did this activity together

Phone shop!

In some words two consonants make one sound, such as **'ph'** in phone.

- How many words can you find that begin with **'sh'**?
- Write them down with your helper.
- How many did you find?

116   Spelling and phonics

impact WRITING HOMEWORK

Tele-tele!

A prefix is a letter or group of letters at the beginning of a word which adjusts its meaning.

'Tele-' is a prefix which came from the Greek for **far away**.

● How many **tele** words can you write down and learn to spell?

Start with: **television**

To the helper:

● Collect as many **tele** words as you can using magazines, books etc... Talk about what the words might mean. For example, **television** might mean something to do with seeing things from far away.

● Practise writing down the spellings together; once your child has learned the 'tele' part, then they will only have to learn the other half of the word each time.

In learning to spell, children have to learn many conventions, and this reveals one of them; that is, by recalling a familiar part of the word, they only have the unfamiliar part to worry about!

_____and
child

_____
helper(s)

did this activity together

Spelling and phonics 117

To the helper:

- Collect as many '**oo**' words as you can using magazines, books or newspapers.
- Can anyone else help you carry on the list?

This activity draws children's attention to specific features of word spellings. It also helps to group words in 'families', for example all those words with a double 'o'.

_____ and
child

_____
helper(s)

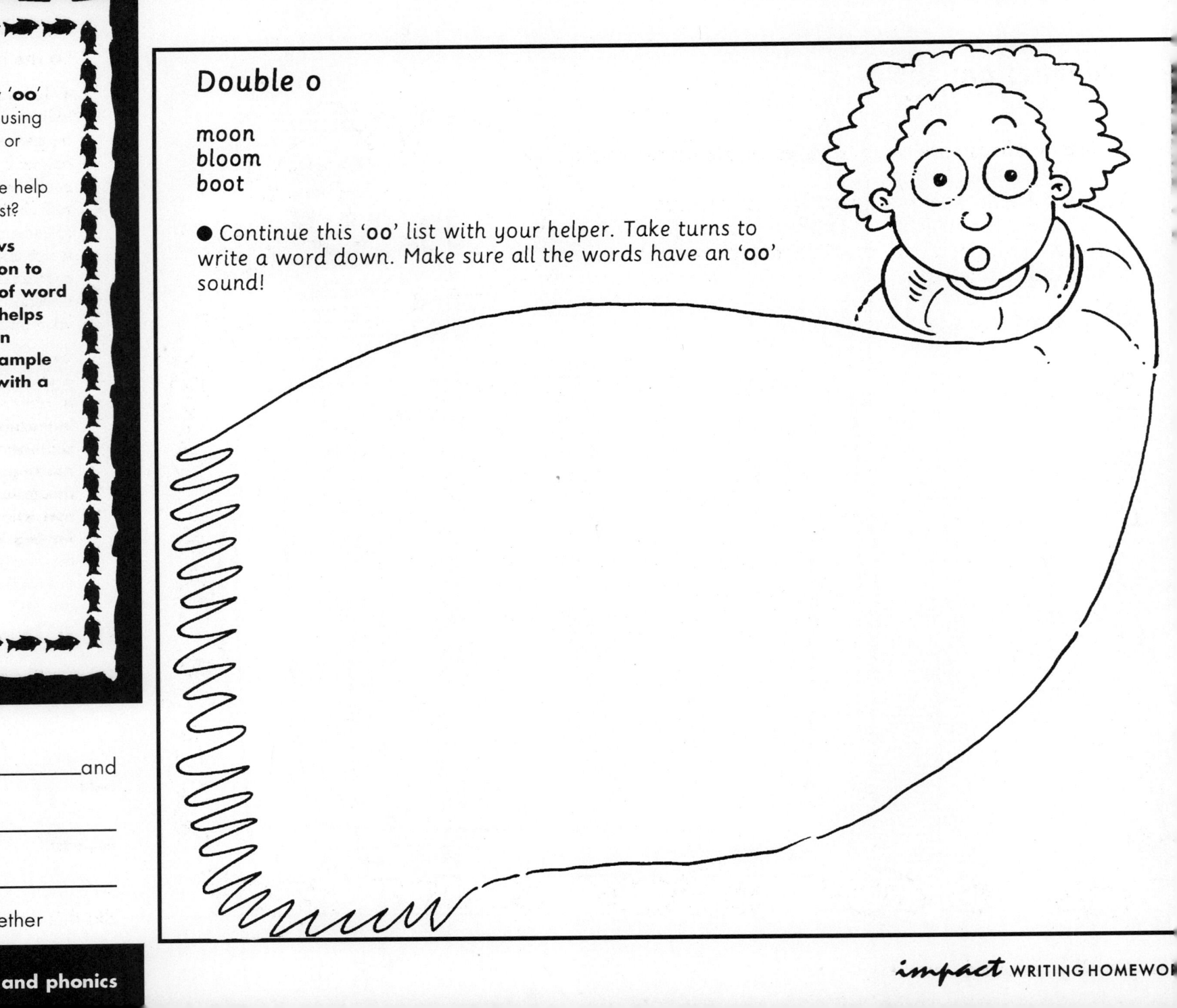

_____
did this activity together

Spelling and phonics

Double o

moon
bloom
boot

● Continue this '**oo**' list with your helper. Take turns to write a word down. Make sure all the words have an '**oo**' sound!

impact WRITING HOMEWORK

Rhyming animals!

Mouse and **louse** are two creatures whose names rhyme.

- Think of some more rhyming pairs of creatures.
- Write them down, and draw some pictures of them.

To the helper:
- Talk together about animals that you can think of; perhaps you have an animal book at home that could help you?
- Talk about how similarly (or differently) the rhyming words are spelled. Let your child start the writing, but do take over once they have had enough.

By isolating a sound, and concentrating on it, the children are far more likely to spot any patterns when they are reading, and even more likely to spell them correctly when they are writing independently.

_____ and
child

_____
helper(s)

did this activity together

impact WRITING HOMEWORK

Spelling and phonics

To the helper:

- Brainstorm as many rhyming words as you can on a scrap piece of paper before you start. Consider using a pet name.
- Let your child write as much as they can, but take over if they start getting tired or frustrated.
- Talk about the rhyming words you have found – do any of them have the same ending?

Recognising rhyming words is important in understanding patterns in words, and might help the children with 'guessing' the spellings of other words when they are writing. We shall enjoy sharing the silly sentences in class.

_____ and

child

_____

helper(s)

_____

did this activity together

Rhyming sentence

● Think of some words that rhyme with your name (or a shortened version of it).

● Write a silly sentence about yourself that uses at least three of them!

For example: '**Jane** writes her **name**, then catches a **train** in the **rain**.'
'**Sam** eats **jam** and **ham** sandwiches in his **pram**.'

● Make the sentence as silly and funny as you want!

120 **Spelling and phonics**

impact WRITING HOMEWOR

Star light, star bright...

Say this rhyme out loud.

**Star light, star bright,
first star I see tonight.
I wish I may,
I wish I might,
have the wish I wish tonight.**

● Can you hear the sound that keeps appearing in this rhyme?

● Write out a rhyme, poem or song with your helper which has a rhyme.

● Underline the parts that rhyme.

To the helper:

● See if your child can spot the repeating '**-ight**' all the way through. Underline it if you want.
● Talk about the songs and rhymes you know, and seetry to find one with lots of rhymes in it.
● Help your child with the writing; but let them do as much as they can.

Recognising rhyming words is important in understanding patterns in words, and might help the children with 'guessing' the spellings of other words when they are writing on their own. We shall enjoy sharing the poems and rhymes the children have found back at school.

_____ and
child

_____
helper(s)

_____
did this activity together

Spelling and phonics 121

To the helper:

- There are often two or three words that trip you up. Most people need to see a word written down before they can tell if they have spelled it correctly, so focus on *looking* at the words to learn them, rather than by chanting out the letters.
- One strategy is 'Look, cover, write, check': the child looks at the word, commits the look of it to memory, covers up the word, tries to write it down from memory, and then checks it. Repeat four or five times.

This activity works on the children's 'stumbling block' spellings, which helps them with their independent writing.

_____ and
child

_____
helper(s)

_____
did this activity together

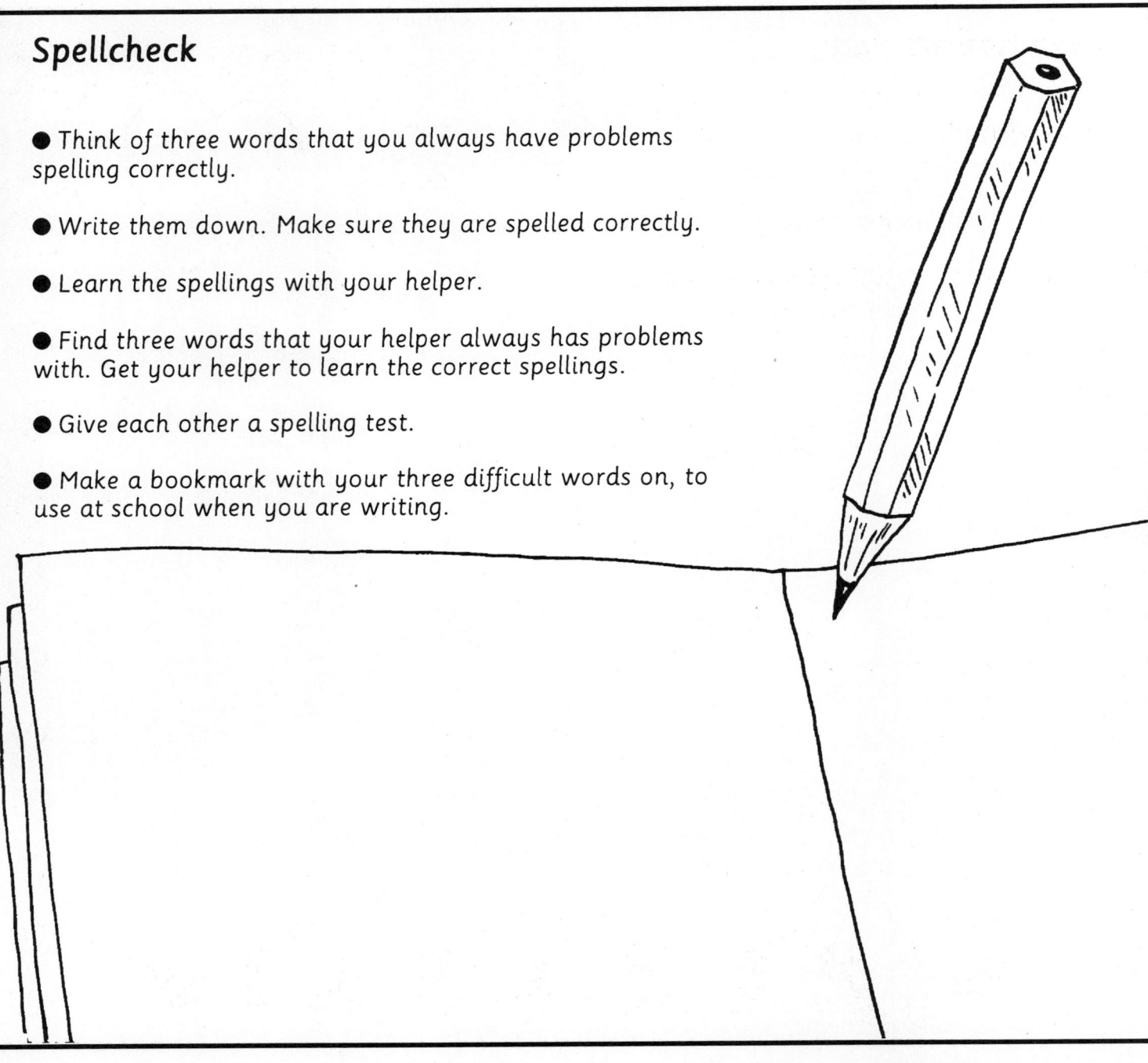

Spellcheck

- Think of three words that you always have problems spelling correctly.

- Write them down. Make sure they are spelled correctly.

- Learn the spellings with your helper.

- Find three words that your helper always has problems with. Get your helper to learn the correct spellings.

- Give each other a spelling test.

- Make a bookmark with your three difficult words on, to use at school when you are writing.

Valentine message

**Roses are red,
Violets are blue...**

- Finish the Valentine message for someone you love!
- Make sure the last word rhymes with **'blue'**.

To the helper:

- Perhaps you could make a few suggestions to start off the activity, so the children get an idea of the kind of thing people write (silly or serious).
- Help with the writing if necessary.

Recognising rhyming words is important in understanding spelling patterns in words, and might help the children with 'guessing' the spellings of other words when they are writing on their own.

_____and

child

_____

helper(s)

_____

did this activity together

Spelling and phonics 123

To the helper:

- This game is based on the game of **Hangman**.
- Choose a word that your child will be able to guess; perhaps a familiar name.
- Take turns to play; after one game your child may be able to do one for you (it might help for them to have the word written down on a secret piece of paper that they can refer to if they need to check any letters).

This game concentrates the children's attention on the positioning of letters within words; and the number of letters in a word. We shall continue with the game at school.

_____and

child

_____

helper(s)

_____

did this activity together

Spelling and phonics

Dragon's teeth

This is a guess-the-word game for two people.

- You have to guess a word one letter at a time.

- Each time your guess is wrong, you must colour in one of the dragon's teeth. When all his teeth are coloured he can bite you! So guess the word as quickly as you can!

- Your helper must think of a name or word you both know how to spell, but they must keep it a secret. He/she must write dashes (- - -) for each letter in the word. You can guess one letter at a time. If you get it right, your helper must fill in that letter in the correct place on the dashes. If the guess was wrong, you must colour in one of the teeth, and write that letter down near to the dragon.

You win if you can guess the word before the dragon bites!

impact WRITING HOMEWORK

Newspaper words

- Cut out ten words from the newspaper. Now paste them on to a piece of paper in alphabetical order.

- Draw a picture to illustrate one of the words.

To the helper:

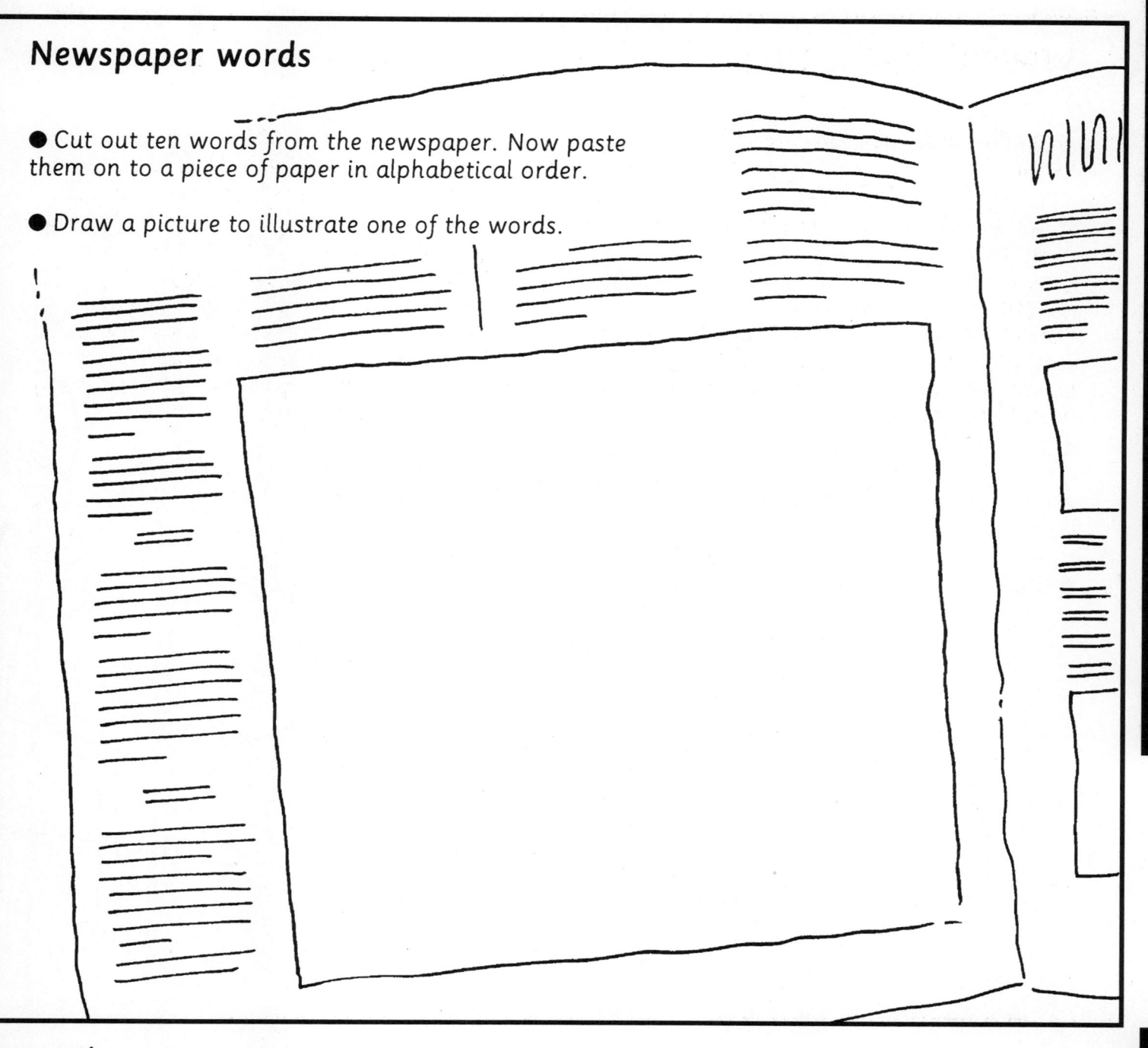

- You will need to help your child read some of the words in the newspaper. They will almost certainly need help in arranging these in alphabetical order. Help by repeating the alphabet with them.

This activity helps children focus on how we put words in alphabetical order. This is a crucial skill in developing dictionary work. We shall also look at the different words the children have selected, and make a complete alphabet of 'newspaper words'.

_____ and
child

_____
helper(s)

did this activity together

Spelling and phonics

To the helper:

● Make sure that the two letters are consecutive in a word.

● Talk about the sound the letters make – sometimes two letters can make a single sound; either by making a new combined sound (as in **-ai**), or if one of them is silent (as in **-mb**).

This activity helps children focus on the structure of words, and provides them with strategies for spelling by recognising letter combinations.

_____ and

child

_____

helper(s)

_____

did this activity together

Spot the missing letters

● Look at these sentences.

• 'It's **r _ _** ning cats and dogs today.'
• 'He was **cli _ _** ing a ladder.'

● They both have two letters missing. Can you fill them in?

● Now make up two sentences of your own, leaving missing letters.

● See if your helper can fill in the missing letters.

● Let them write two sentences with missing letters for you to complete.

● Bring some more into school ready for your friends to try.

126 **Spelling and phonics**

impact WRITING HOMEWO

More than one!

Many words become plural simply by adding an 's'. But some don't!

- Talk about some of the oddest or more unusual plurals that you can think of. Write a short list – be sure to spell them correctly!

To the helper:

- Discuss the ways in which some words become plural – other than by adding an **'s'**. For example, Mouse – mice. Why isn't it house, hice?! Are there any patterns you can see?

This activity helps us to think about the structure and spelling of certain words. It also focuses on those words which are the exception rather than the rule.

_____and
child

_____
helper(s)

_____
did this activity together

Spelling and phonics

IMPACT schools

We are trying to compile a list of IMPACT schools so that we can:
- inform you as new materials are produced;
- offer help and support via our INSET office;
- find out the spread of this type of shared writing homework.

Also, because it is helpful if you have support and advice when starting up a shared homework scheme, we have a team of registered in-service trainers around Britain. Through the IMPACT office we can arrange for whole day, half day or 'twilight' sessions in schools.

I would like further information about IMPACT INSET sessions.

YES/NO

Please photocopy and cut off this strip and return it to:

The IMPACT Office,
Education Dept.,
University of North London,
Holloway Road,
London N7 8DB.
0171 753 7052

Teacher's name _____
School's name _____
_____
Address _____
_____
_____
LEA _____

Management

Most teachers send the shared writing task as a photocopied sheet included in the children's **Reading Folder** or in their IMPACT **Maths folder**. Remind the children that they may use the back of the IMPACT sheet to write on. Before the activity is sent home, it is crucial that the teacher prepares the children for the task. This may involve reading a story, going over some ideas or having a group or class discussion. Some ideas are provided here in the Teachers' Notes for each activity. The importance of this preparation cannot be overstressed.

Many of the tasks done at home lend themselves naturally to a display or enable the teacher to make a class-book. A shared writing display board in the entrance hall of the school gives parents an important sense that their work at home is appreciated and valued.

The shared writing activity sheets can be stuck into an exercise book kept specifically for this purpose. Any follow-up work that the children do in school can also be put into this book. As the books go back and forth with the activity sheets this enables parents to see how the work at home has linked to work in class.

Non-IMPACTers

We know that parental support is a key factor in children's education and children who cannot find anyone with whom to share the writing task may be losing out. Try these strategies:
- Encourage, cajole and reward the children who bring back their shared writing. If a child – and parent/carer – does the task haphazardly, praise the child whenever the task is completed, rather than criticise if it does not.
- If possible, invite a couple of parents in to share the activities with the children. This involves parents in the life of the school as well as making sure that some children don't lose out.
- Some schools set up 'writing partners' between children in two different classes pairing a child from Y6 with a child in Y1 for shared writing activities, perhaps weekly or fortnightly.

None of these strategies is perfect, but many parents will help when they can and with encouragement, will join in over the longer term.

Useful information and addresses

The IMPACT shared maths scheme is running successfully in thousands of schools in the UK and abroad. The shared writing works in the same way, and obviously complements the maths very well. Both fit in with the shared reading initiatives (PACT or CAPER) which most schools in the country also run. The OFSTED Inspection Schedules require and take account of schools working with parents as well as focusing on the quality of teaching and learning. IMPACT continues to receive positive mentions in inspectors' reports.

Further information about the IMPACT Project and IMPACT inservice training for schools or parents' groups can be obtained from: The IMPACT Project, School of Teaching Studies, University of North London, 166–220 Holloway Road, London N7 8DB.

The Shared Maths Homework books can be obtained from Scholastic Publications, Westfield Road, Southam, Nr Leamington Spa, Warwickshire CV33 0JH.

For IMPACT Diaries contact: IMPACT Supplies, PO Box 126 Witney, Oxfordshire OX8 5YL. Tel: 01993 774408.

IMPACT: Imaginative Writing: Key Stage One/Scottish Levels A-B

The activities in this book support the following requirements for writing in the UK national curricula for English.

National Curriculum: English
1. Range - a,b,c
2. Key Skills - a,d
3. Standard English and Language Study - a,b

Scottish 5-14 Guidelines: English Language	
Strand	Level
Spelling	A/B
Knowledge about language	B

Northern Ireland Curriculum: English
Within meaningful contexts, pupils should be taught:
- conventional ways of forming letter shapes in upper and lower case;
- the names and order of the letters of the alphabet;
- to spell a range of words recognisably.